The Unseen World
Afterlife Research

by Ryan O'Neill

Published by

BeulA**ithris**
Publishing

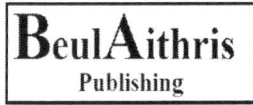

Greenock Scotland

Copyright © by Ryan O'Neill

First Edition Published 2018

ISBN 9781719860208

Contents

Acknowledgements...1

Introduction..3

The Non-Physical Worlds..12

  1. We Are Non-Physical..12
  2. Out Of Body Experience (OBE) 19
  3. Near Death Experience (NDE)...............................24

Researching the Unseen..32

  4. Types Of Afterlife Activity...............................32
  5. A-Z of Paranormal Definitions 41
  6.   Methods For Afterlife Research.........................60
  7.   Analysis & Post Investigation...........................76
  8. Haunted Castles 83

    Aberdour Castle 83
    Blackness Castle 85
    Glamis Castle...88
    Hailes Castle 91
    Norham Castle...93

  9. Religious Haunts 97

    Balmerino Abbey...97
    Cambuskenneth Abbey....................................99
    Kirk O'Shotts 103
    Greyfriars Kirkyard 105

  10. Interesting Haunts 108

    Jedburgh Castle Jail 108
    Mary Kings Close.......................................111
    Mercure Perth Hotel 115
    The Pearce Institute 118

Ruthven Barracks 121

11. Recap of Information & 124
Additional Information 124

Resources 126
About The Author 127

Acknowledgements

I have a lot of people to thank and without their input, support and prompting, I would never have taken on this project, compiling together information into such a book that can be used by others in their own truth seeking.

Starting with my wife, Carrie, who has supported me in everything I have done. She has urged me on to follow my passion and continue the seeking of truth in this topic. Carrie is often with me at locations, listening to my ideas and gives me the feedback I require to push on. Behind every man is a great woman it's said, and in this case, it can be no more accurate. Thank you, Carrie.

Let us not forget my kids Tammy, Katelynn, Kane & Rhian. All of whom have been on location with me, and even sometimes letting me know the newest cool things that can be done online in this technology and information age.

All of my family and friends have had a hand at one point or another in helping me reach certain goals, such as this book, and every single one are appreciated and thanked.

I have too many names to mention in the paranormal field, I have learned from them all as I see myself as a student with many teachers.

I need to single out Greg Stewart for giving me the final boost to get writing, my brainstorming buddy and a damn fine author to boot.
Ally Reid for pushing me with amazing ideas and the Scottish Paranormal team for their professional work, personal growth within the topic of consciousness and their ability to expand their awareness in the topic without fear or favour.

Mark Turner, my Spiritual Guru is another who has helped me stay grounded and yet connected in a spiritual sense.

All my ten thousand plus Haunted Scotland friends on Facebook deserve mention too, the constant feedback, support and ideas they share is out of this world.

Finally, my Dad, Patrick O'Neill, who sadly passed away on 4th of March 2017, he never got a chance to see me finish the book but he did know I was heading in that direction.

Constantly he would urge me to get writing, get busy and to do it now and not wait for time to pass me by, and I'm sad that he is not here to see the finished article, but comfortable enough that he is looking over us all.

This book is dedicated to my Dad, till I see him again which inevitably I shall.

Patrick O'Neill - 2nd September 1959 - 4th March 2017

Introduction

So how does a random person from the east coast of Scotland get involved in the paranormal at such an advanced level? From Kirkcaldy, in the kingdom of Fife, I travel the UK to appear in shows such as Most Haunted, or even end up in Jamaica at the infamous Rose Hall Mansion. We need to go back to the age of three, or thereabouts, as the mind is sketchy about the more delicate details but not the actual event itself. You see, back at such a young age where most people have no recall of situations or events, I have a very vivid memory of paranormal activity transpiring directly above my bedroom cot. Picture the scene: put into your cot for the evening, while it is still light outside and happily drifting into a comfortable sleep. Then BANG, its night time and very dark indeed...

I can see one of those old digital bedside radio clocks, the numbers radiating back towards me. It was beside my Dad's bed, but as my Dad was not with me at this time, I'm assuming it must still have been early evening. Wait, what is that? Up to the left of the clock, I see something moving across the wall: it's a shadowy blob, pulsating and moving. Hold on - there are more coming from different directions and moving towards me, uh oh this is not good, I am getting a little scared here. They form above my head into one giant circular blob.

It is pulsating and moving in an up and down fashion. I try to hit it away with my hands, willing and intending it to go away and leave me alone. I begin to scream. I want my Dad... The door flies open, the light comes on, and the large blobby energy has disappeared into the ether. My Dad picks me up and cuddles me. I have no way to tell him what I saw: it is frustrating and even if I could, would he believe me?

The house we lived in was my grandmothers. My Dad had not long split up from my Mum, and we were temporarily living there, in the back bedroom, which overlooked some garages. My Grandfather had passed away two years previously in the same house. There were plenty of complaints about the house being strange from my aunties and uncles, who had all lived here at one point. Had I tapped into those energies? Was it a ball of consciousness rather than a full manifestation I had seen?

When I told my Dad whole story later in life, one summer evening as we sat with a few alcoholic beverages, he was stunned at my full description of the room, its layout, and the garages seen out of the back window next to my cot. I had reawakened his memory of the room, but he said it was impossible for me to remember such detail. When you experience a unique event, however, it etches itself into your memory; such was the power of the experience... This event was not the only early ghostly occurrence I was to experience.

We now fast forward to the age of thirteen, where, being the bad boy I was, I was skiving off school at a friend of a friend's house and was about to have my worldview shaken to its core. How would you act if faced with blatant paranormal activity, especially if it was happening at the young age of thirteen? Would you think that you were hallucinating, that it could not possibly be happening? I mean, after all, we are conditioned to believe that the afterlife does not exist, while discounting millions of witness reports.

Good job the above happened with three people then. One person was fifteen years old and the other, a year above me at just fourteen years old. I am at this point going to change their names, to protect their identity. Not that Arnold, the fifteen-year-old who lived at the house with his parents, or Watty, my good buddy who lived near me, would mind in the slightest knowing them.

It is a place where I should not have been anyway - I ought to have been the high school learning stuff and not watching the football on Arnolds TV. It was the first and only time I had been in his house; nothing was ever mentioned about the background of the property, until the occurrences began and even then, I was in utter disbelief at what was unfolding before my very eyes. Therefore, It Begins.

My friend Watty had asked to use the toilet, and then departed briefly while I spoke with Arnold, watching and listening to the football, which was now in full swing. When Watty came back into the living room, with a gasp, he was white as a ghost with a rather puzzled look radiating from him.

"Arnold, do you have a ghost or something? I was in the toilet, and something was moving around outside the door!"

When Arnold said yes, and that they had lived with it for years, we let out a chuckle.

Arnold looked cross with us. "Watch this, then." He replied.

He then proceeded to turn off the TV and told us to keep quiet. Within mere minutes, we heard someone walk and shuffle across the floor above us. I immediately thought Arnold had someone else in and said so. I mean, surely he had a family member in or a friend hiding and playing tricks on us all?

He countered me, "Let's go upstairs then; I can show you no one is in and let you experience what we do first hand."

My first thoughts were, if we are going up the stairs, I am in the middle, as this is freaky stuff - someone is either going to jump out at us, or I am about to meet the ghost. We were halfway up the stairs when an almighty crash came from his little sister's room. We all ran in to find his little sisters piggy bank smashed across the floor; I began looking under beds as I was still in such shock. I could not accept what was transpiring. At this point, I had enough, and already decided that this was me finished with such stuff, but, as we descended the stairs, we heard the dogs howl from outside. Arnold had glass doors in his kitchen, leading outside and there were large German Shepherds out in that garden area. This was from where the dogs were and from what we were about to see a situation in which, it had reached the time to leave...

The dogs were scratching the door to get in and going crazy. That was not the problem though, oh no, the problem happened to be that every single cupboard door on the wall or under bunker was fully open. Something had done this and very fast indeed, Something non-physical. We decided to leave, but as we prepared to do so, we still asked Arnold more questions.

He was very calm about the whole situation you see, because he had lived with it for so long, and whatever it was, it had never harmed him at all. He even knew who it was, an elderly gentleman that happen I remember living in my village. The old man had walked with the same step and shuffle we heard upstairs, when we were still in the living room. . He had passed away in the house before Arnold's family had bought it. Seemingly, he was in no hurry to move on into the spirit world that was for sure. Kettles switching on and off, noises, footsteps and other similar phenomena were a daily occurrence to Arnold and his family.

Every time I think about the paranormal or hear people dismissing others' experiences as either imagination or wishful thinking, I think back to this activity, witnessed by three individuals who were alone in a house with nothing to gain or lose from such retelling of the story. I then smile. People are entitled to their opinion but need to ensure they study before making conclusions.

My aunt always said that I attracted spirits; the reason being is I have always tended to find myself in situations that defy logic or reality as conditioned into us from a young age. Little subtle cues in the environment, whether an unmistakable cold spot following me around or physical phenomenon, such as mirrors and pictures blatantly moving in front of my family members and me. There was nothing subtle about this next activity, however. Oh no, this one would rock me to my very core.

Physical Activity by Non-Physical Energies.

The build-up of negative energy seemed enough to trigger an almighty case of paranormal activity. Looking back, the house, where I lived alone, was already subject to unusual occurrences. I would come home to find the TV on when I knew it was turned off before going to work.

There was a sense of not being alone in the small one bedroom bottom flat, in Normand Road, Dysart. Small instances were brushed off as me being forgetful, or perhaps imagination and such other excuses to try to cover-up the unusual paranormal activity occurring at the flat in Dysart.. The breaking point was after a negative event in life, one that had me running for a bottle of alcohol to dull the senses and cope with disappointment and hurt.

I had split with a short-term girlfriend in a hurtful way; I was cheated on, and there was nothing I could do about it. The venting to friends that evening – allowing the energy to build up in the house – threw it all into rather a peculiar territory, as within the twelve hours, my viewpoint on reality was to shift yet again. It was always as if at key points in my life, I was to be shaken by some greater unknown power. At the time, it was only classified as a shocking experience.

The morning after the night before: on awakening, the first noticeable event was that a bedside lamp I had left on was now off! Ah, blown bulb I thought until I went to click the lamp switch as you do and on it came. This indeed was highly confusing. Oh well, I thought, let's stick that in my continued excuses of forgetful memory - until I entered the living room and witnessed a catalogue of physical events that scared me.

The TV had apparently moved to a side on position, ornaments were all on top of it, and various items were transferred all over the living room and adjoining kitchen. The kitten's cat litter was now sitting in the middle of the kitchen floor under a stool, which, incidentally had been moved to that position as I looked around, I be in complete shock and disbelief. I thought I had been burgled – surely, someone had broken into through the window or door, which was the prevailing, thought now running through my alarmed mind. I checked all windows and doors...all locked!

I sat quietly trying to understand what had happened, not thinking of paranormal activity. You see, this was before I started my research in that area. My cat – which had been running around – stopped, began to look over my shoulder and then started to hiss while arching her back! Then I knew, as the hairs on my neck stood up and the cold shivers brushed over my body, I was in the middle of real paranormal activity.

Remember, this was while only eighteen years old and nowhere near the knowledge base or extensive experience I have now... I stood up and walked out the door to gather my thoughts and calm down my fear; everything seemed so surreal at this point. I did return within fifteen minutes, and began the clean up. I was clearly on edge at this point.

Help Was Required!

I stayed in the house for a further month or two before finally leaving. Light bulbs would blow, items would move, and I always felt as if I was being watched. I got in contact with a good medium from Edinburgh– her name escapes me now – and she attended the house with two friends to help. Working on only fuel money – thankfully, as I was rather poor at the time – she began to give us information on the active spirit, which was resident in the flat. The medium told us he was an ex-miner who used to live in these old houses and he did not even know he was in spirit.

The activity with the TV, electrics and likewise was a result of him trying to gain attention from me, as I moved around within what he deemed as still his home. They helped him pass over that evening, but by this time, the surreal reality of it all had already seeped into me, and I was very uncomfortable now. However, the seed was firmly planted, and my destiny was set.

There are only so many mystical experiences a person can have before they seek answers, find out who else has gone through the same, and then start digging. . It may have taken a few more years to get going, but those answers would be sought as I created Scottish Paranormal.

Paranormal Researcher, Observer & Truth Seeker

I made contacts all over the world, as in order to seek the truth, you have to open up to those who have the experience to help you. Whether it be friends such as Barry Fitzgerald - before his fantastic TV years - or members of the TAPS family in the USA who I frequently shared brainstorming sessions with, I would keep digging into this topic. My absolute obsession with the mystical side of life would have me working on material for up to sixteen hours a day, every day with no breaks. I spent every penny I had on equipment, travel and online resources to aid me in my learning, research and seeking.

I am blessed to have a wife who supported me at every step of the way; she knew how important it was for me, and for that, I will always be grateful. Where some would dip their toes into the topic, I would dive in head first and beyond my comfort zones. As said, I was utterly obsessed, and this reflected in my work. It was something that was picked up on by the Scottish Media, TV companies, radio stations and my colleagues the world over.

It was not all plain sailing, however, the more exposure I had with this work, the more I would attract sceptics or those, who for reasons only known to themselves, were jealous of the work I was pushing out over many platforms .Personally, I was in it for one reason, the truth and nothing was going to stop me.. During those amazing years of research with my friends from within the local community, we uncovered a lot of evidence, a lot of fun and a lot of hard work was put in place.

My contact list grew, and I was assisting large production companies such as Antix Productions - makers of Most Haunted - behind the scenes. I would regularly be contacted for Scottish research, suggesting locations and providing stories and witness reports .It was around this time I would be asked to take part in Most Haunted Live, from Edinburgh, in 2006. It was a hard decision to make, as honestly, I was not a person who had ever dealt with TV work or public speaking.

I was from Kirkcaldy, Fife, a place where we tend to speak with a strong, fast accent. How would anyone understand me? This would put a massive amount of pressure on me. However, I did, agree to take part, as I rarely would refuse a situation where I could learn to grow personally. If I wanted to mingle with those who knew more than I did in this area did, I would have to remove my fears and go for it.

The audience would be filled with colleagues such as Mark Turner of GhostFinders Scotland, someone who is a close friend and I admire, and also The Ghostfinder General Jimmy Devlin. He was an excellent researcher who was bringing the topic to the public in such a worthy manner in Edinburgh. So, it was a yes, let's get through there and surround myself with people who vibrate on a similar level to what I was trying to achieve in the search.

Inside I was scared: one thousand members of the public were in the Usher Hall, our live studio. I was to sit with my friend Ewan Irvine, a very able Scottish medium, on the couch with Paul Ross, the presenter. How I got through that I will never know, I was buzzing afterwards for sure, but being beamed out live across the UK and America, how did I get to this position? The messages poured in from all over America; my colleagues had seen me live and were congratulating me. Some struggled with the accent but were overjoyed to see me on their TV screens.

After this I would go on to appear in various TV shows such as Tough Gig with Arabella Weir, Most Haunted down at Coalhouse Fort in England and lately USA Hit TV show Brew Dogs. I recall in 2008 when I got the email from Antix Productions asking if I could forward my mobile number to them. They needed to call me about Most Haunted, and it was rather urgent.

I had a rough idea what they were about to ask, as the rumour was that a new series had been commissioned for Living TV. They would need assistance on set or with some research on locations. The call came in; I was asked if I knew of any good parapsychologists, as regular Ciaran O'Keeffe had just become a Dad and was busy with his partner and new family. My initial thoughts were to forward them onto the Edinburgh University Koester Unit, where a world-renowned department of such individuals were heavily involved in Parapsychological research. If they were going to do it right, what better place to recruit experts from?

It was at this point they said it was me they preferred, and what were my thoughts on helping out on two shows? This was a hard one for me. I had helped them so much in the past, and they had always looked after me with respect and kindness. However, within the actual field of paranormal research, they were viewed differently from how the public perceived them.

It was a very popular show with the public, and although most will not admit it, several researchers first got interested in watching such shows, drawn to the historical locations and possibilities of evidence of the afterlife. Still, grumbles did come from more sceptical researchers and large sceptic organisations about Most Haunted. So for the sake of my own networking and seeking of the truth, I would need to be cautious and honest, bluntly so.

I agreed to fill in for Ciaran, as long as I could call it as I see it. The producers were very much happy with this; they said expected nothing less. I flew down to London, got a taxi to Coalhouse Fort - a fair distance - and looked after by Yvette, Karl and the team for my duration of stay across the border. I thoroughly enjoyed the experience, I held my own integrity, and in the aftermath, I was contacted by many sceptics who also congratulated me on my realness.

My only regret was my nervousness about the cameras and new experience I was going through, which, in hindsight is something I would approach differently today. Experience does that though, you learn and grow, and back then, I lacked such an experience in media. I am always asked if I saw fraud, and I have to say I did not, nothing was faked in front of me. Please do remember I was focused on the perceived activity, walking with Yvette and Johnnie and taking in all the information being provided.

Lots of footage also never made it to the show. We had such great possibilities with the Thermal Imager in the dark tunnels that night. A couple of camera operators and I followed cold spots through the tunnels, being hit with blasts of freezing air and getting really interesting data. The show only had an hour and lots of footage just never made it off the cutting room floor. I have to say, some of the really interesting stuff never made it to the public for whatever reason.

All the above was in the name of promoting the paranormal topic and in particular, the afterlife and hauntings. Throughout all this, however, I would not forget that the main aim was to find some personal experiences of the afterlife. As my granny used to say, "what's meant for you will not pass you by" and throughout my time on this subject, I've been blessed to have had some excellent opportunities to share what I've uncovered.

I've not gone seeking any fame and certainly not a fortune, as I've spent a fair whack on the afterlife research. I've taken each day as it comes, each request with seriousness and kept visualising what I want to achieve in my search. No longer do I need to prove anything to anyone as I have an inner knowing that we carry on after death. I've had my proof: My evidence and my experiences. It's my wish for others to have theirs now too, which is the whole reason why I am writing this book.

I want to take you with me, allow you to see, hear and feel for yourself the wonders of the non-physical. In order to do this, I will need to show you how the non-physical contact us, how we have not been told the whole truth about reality and show you exactly how to gain your own experiences without the need to pay others or take information on blind faith.

This book is constructed in three parts to achieve the above. Firstly, I would like to talk about the non-physical world, the not so physical world we live in and shine a light on consciousness, that hard problem for science that is fundamental to everything. After this, in section two of the book, I will share everything I know about researching the unseen. This will include definitions, apparitions and methodologies to get you started in your seeking. I will then end with a full section showing unique locations I've personally investigated - you can do so too - and what I found at each one of these places I had the privilege to wander alone, and with my team at Scottish Paranormal. Let's get started.

The Non-Physical Worlds

1. We Are Non-Physical

I would calculate that I've conducted over eight years of research into the big questions in life. The main question is why we are here and how does that fit within the afterlife and unseen world? It's safe to say that in order to conduct my own research, and categorise my experiences with the paranormal, I would need to stand on the shoulders of giants in areas with which, I was less knowledgeable. This is where I introduce you to a marvellous researcher and scientist, Tom Campbell, someone who I've recommended to a plethora of fellow seekers throughout the years. I've done my background checks on Tom, watched hundreds of hours' worth of videos on his theory, and marvelled at his adventures outside this reality with the evidence to back it up.

So how does a NASA Physicist come up with a theory of everything, which is soaked in the spiritual? Thomas Warren Campbell is a scientist, lecturer, and author of the *My Big T.O.E.* (Theory of Everything) trilogy, a work that unifies general relativity, metaphysics and not forgetting Quantum Physics, along with the hard problem of consciousness. Tom's work is based on the simulation argument, which shows that reality is subjective.

Tom received his master's degree in Physics in 1968, before commencing his PhD program specialisation in Experimental Nuclear Physics. During the time of the extended study, Tom decided to enrol in a Transcendental Meditation (TM) class, which he was very successful with, a technique he then goes on to suggest helped identify errors in his computer code while working for the US Army Intelligence later in his career. Coincidentally, as Tom was opening up his mind to meditation, one of his supervisors brought his attention to a book authored by Bob Munroe, which described a bigger reality obtained through Outer Body Experiences. Tom was asked what he thought of Bob's claims and ultimately was invited out to Bob's home with other fellow scientists for a tour and talk. Upon learning that Bob Monroe was looking for scientists to help him study altered states of consciousness in the hope to legitimise what he was experiencing, Campbell applied for the position immediately and subsequently began working with Bob at Monroe Laboratories.

Tom always said that if there was more to this reality, he wanted to know all about it. His only request was he wished to be shown how to go out of the body by Bob Munroe. Tom believes his research with Bob helped solidify many of his discoveries, insights and hypothesises into the nature of reality and the mechanics of what he terms "the larger consciousness system".

The Larger Consciousness System

Some call it God, Allah or Source, while others refer to it as the Creator or perhaps the Tao or Brahman. Regardless of what metaphor or title you use, there is little doubt that there is a fundamental energy to life, its consciousness. Tom calls this "The Larger Consciousness System" something we are all part of and growing together as. It is an evolving system of consciousness, with each one of us being an individualised point of consciousness looking to evolve in order to assist the whole. The Ancients would say, "We are all one," and really, this is what they speak of. It is a paradox – we are all experiencing reality as an awareness, yet we are also part of the one big picture of consciousness, which is also evolving, due to our endeavours here.

As I previously mentioned, Tom was shown how to go out of the body by Bob Munroe as part of the agreement to build a laboratory to study Outer Body Experiences, which Bob was frequently having. It was during this time that Tom would get the solid subjective proof he needed with regards to these explorations, taking them from what might be classed as merely imagination or dreaming to the concrete evidence that he not only left his physical body, but that he did so jointly in company of another scientist. Although Tom and the other participants at the lab were gaining fantastic evidence with regards to the ability to separate consciousness from the physical body by going into altered states, nothing quite solidifies such that a joint experience.

During one experiment, while Tom was in his own isolation booth, his headset on and a microphone above his head - Bob had taught them to narrate their experiences to record it to tape - his fellow scientist Dennis Mennerich was likewise in his booth preparing to shoot off into the non-physical realms. When they had completed this session, they made their way up to Bob's office for a debriefing. Bob was apparently sitting with a very big grin on his face

"So you think you were together out of the body?" Bob asked.

Tom replied, "It would appear so."

It was at this point that Bob played both tape recorders simultaneously, and what came back via the audio was astonishing. Tom and Dennis have described and experienced the same things: they were together out of the body, doing the tests and explaining what they were encountering. Evidence of it being real was now firmly planted in their minds. No longer was it mere statistics on paper; this was the reality. Tom said he just kept saying to himself for around two weeks "Oh my, it's real" as the gravity of the situation hit him: a fully qualified physicist had experienced the nonphysical. There was a bigger picture.

Since those early days, Tom has continued to go out of the body by altering his consciousness - something we can all do - and has built an excellent model of reality. He explains fully how we are all consciousness, the fundamentals and everything else is just information. We make choices in life, and these choices will determine whether we grow and evolve spiritually or we devolve. We have free will, it's our choice, and if you are interested, I would certainly suggest you grab Tom's book and begin studying. It is outside the scope of this book to go too deeply into this work. I only wish to highlight the research into consciousness - what we truly are, and how we can communicate with the unseen.

Tom's Research into Death

Tom has been asked several times about the death process and has gone on to explain his understanding of it through his Outer Body Experience explorations and witnessing what was happening. Remember Tom is a scientist, and whilst he was in these altered states of consciousness, the scientific mind-set did not cease. He wanted to know how everything worked so he could explain what happens when we die. Tom talks about different realities as being frames: so we have the dreaming reality frame, the transition frame for when we die and reality frames we can visit when in the Outer Body state.

Our dearly departed go into this transitional frame on the point of physical death, then from there they will move on in their spiritual growth, either to reincarnate back here in the physical realm - or other physical type frames - or they may hang in what we term the non-physical. However, whatever frame we are in, it seems to be physical to us, much like when you are in a dream. Where that focus is, as you are acutely aware of your surroundings, it will always seem physical to you. When you die, you go into a reality frame that is different from the dreaming reality. As mentioned above, it is not the same as the Outer Body frame that you can access either; you go into another reality frame that was made especially for people who are just transitioning from this reality frame to another.

Great care is taken with these transitions of consciousness purely due to the confusion experienced when one dies. To find yourself fully aware in another place with no ills, pains or worries is said to be highly confusing and at times stressful to the consciousness, which has transitioned. Your physical body dies and then suddenly you're somewhere else, much like falling asleep and waking up in another place all of a sudden. You tend to be a little stressed and confused as to where you are and what is going on. It is while in this transitional reality frame that you are met by loved ones and other beings who have the sole purpose of calming you down, explaining to you what's happening and keeping you stress-free during the process. If you have a powerful belief system, that belief system will become a hook by which they will manipulate you to get you to relax in this reality frame, ensuring you let go of the process that you have just experienced.

This is why the stories you hear of people who've been through the Near Death Experience phenomena are so different. Some may see Jesus, Buddha or beings in long robes, while others may see loved ones or people they have known who passed over a long time ago. Whatever beliefs you hold, they will be used to help you ease in this reality frame immediately after death. It's all about calming you down and allowing you to move on to the next phase of your growth. Some pseudo-sceptics have used the above to hit back at NDE's as a only being a product of the brain. They will ask how come only religious people see religious figures, and will then go on to proclaim that it's all just in the mind and that this is proof of such.

They are both right and wrong in their assertions: right in that a person's sincere held beliefs will impact on what they immediately experience in the reality frame the individual will transition to following death. However, the sceptics are wrong in their conclusions. They have approached it entirely from a materialistic stance, with little understanding of the process, which I have just written about. Tom talks about this in depth in many of his videos; he even explains that the toughest transitions he has seen - yes he has watched the process unfold, as have others - was that of people who were highly religious. They struggled with the process due to the differences between what they had been indoctrinated in during this life and the actual experience. Likewise for those who were involved in sudden deaths or accidents.

This swings me back around to my own research into the paranormal and sightings of religious figures at many sites I've visited. I came to a conclusion long ago that the extremely high amount of sightings of monks, priests and nuns, to name a few, must have a cause and most likely those who do wander, were scared to transition and had somehow remained here in this reality frame. I speak about this in many location files, some of which also feature in this book.

We Are All Consciousness, Even the Spirit We Seek

The fundamental truth is this: we are all consciousness here in this reality frame trying our best to grow the quality we possess. However, as we know, no one has actually told us this while growing up, we've been led to believe that we are here to learn, work and then die into nothing! This stance is not to our benefit and only really benefits those who may profit from our lifestyles. If we all knew the above - and some do instinctively - we certainly would approach life differently for sure.

The very essence that is within us is within everyone you see and every creature too. Anything that is aware and making choices is conscious, and doing what they need to do in order to grow their inner quality. We are all playing the same game here, yet not many people know they are actually playing it. Let's not forget, the communication work we do with the unseen, actually is connecting with other forms of consciousness - out with non-sentient hauntings - so a level of respect is needed, much like the respect afforded to our peers.

We Are All Netted

At a deep level within us, we are all netted with other forms of consciousness, linked at such a level that conscious communication is not the be all and end all here. Let me give you an example: if you think of a person and then they call, do you call it coincidence? If you think of a long lost friend and he or she bumps into you shortly after, is this a coincidence?

Do you have a connection with your partner, perhaps you sing a song, and they tell you they were just doing with the same song in their head. You may finish off each other's sentences; decide on actions together at same time. This is a high-netted connection through consciousness. You really must stop looking at everything as mere coincidences and begin to understand that the very essence of you - and others - are connected at a profound level. Now let's go deeper into this for the sake of the book here, and what we are trying to dig into with regards to afterlife investigating and the unseen worlds.

If we are netted, connected and communicating at our root with other forms of consciousness, what about during our research, investigation and observations into the afterlife? Would, for example, a dismissive attitude towards the non-physical lead to any such consciousness being to form the opinion that it is not worth bothering to communicate? Would the simple intentions of our mind be the deciding factor on how successful we were in communication with the afterlife? I will suggest YES, the biggest detriment I've found to paranormal research and investigation was intentions that were dismissive of any such phenomena. Not always, I would say, but in a high probability nonetheless. So be careful of those intentions and inner conversations.

To summarise the above information is to say, that fundamentally, we are all consciousness and that is all there is. It is an essence that survives in everything that has awareness and can make choices.

Our consciousness can leave our body through practice - or sometimes spontaneously - which backs up the data that we can survive outside the physical human body. People such as Tom Campbell, Bob Munroe and a plethora of other scientists and academics have provided evidence of these events in consciousness, some of which, we will discuss later to give a basic understanding of what we are actually dealing with here. You see, we are dealing with consciousness, in the afterlife and in the physical and if we can understand this, we can elevate our communication with the unseen worlds.

2. Out Of Body Experience (OBE)

I'm going to start this section by revealing some private information that I have not released into the public domain. There are many reasons I did not reveal it, mostly due to it being private experimentation, but also due to how far out it sounded for my online followers and friends. I completed some intense research into OBEs, the techniques needed to navigate the unseen world you enter and the practice you need to put into place to induce this altered state of consciousness. I studied people such as Tom Campbell, Bob Munroe, William Buhlman, Ryan Cropper and Charlie Morley to name but a few. I took what I had learned and started to practice every afternoon for a two hour period. I was primarily using Binaural Beats for this practice and luckily learned the tell-tale signs of when I was about to induce the OBE.

I say lucky because if I never knew about the noises, intense vibration feeling and sleep paralysis stages, I would have freaked out a little and stopped what was about to be an awe-inspiring moment. One second I was lying comfortably on my back, listening to the tones of the audio through the stereo headset, then I perhaps drifted a tad into a void and close to sleep. The next thing I knew, I was vibrating heavily within, whooshing sounds, body paralysed yet this energetic vibration getting more and more intense.

The sounds inside my head were also intensifying to a level I find hard to explain. I was calm. However, I knew exactly what was about to happen due to my research, so I said to myself "Just go with it", and I am so glad that I did. Everything stopped, and a silence comforted me, I was no longer in the physical body on the bed, I was somehow drifting above the bed as pure awareness. I felt absolutely amazing in this state of consciousness, so free and very much aware of everything. I knew my body was on the bed below me; I knew I was what I could only describe as floating above it, I heard every noise of the room, outside and in the house. I was ecstatic that I had managed to do what all these great consciousness explorers had told us to do. I was giggling in my altered form; I was also so happy that everything I was researching was proving to be very real indeed. It gave me a new perspective on afterlife research and our roles here on earth.

The experience lasted about 5 minutes I would guess, a little fear did enter at the end when I thought to myself "Ok Ryan, time to go back in" I just wanted to get everything down on paper before I forgot what I had just been through too. So do I believe in OBEs? No, I do not believe it's real, I know it's real. You see, there is no substitute for real first-hand experience, compared to the opinions of so-called experts with qualifications attached to their name. They may give you fanciful explanations which are far more crazy that the reality of it all.

I will always advocate that people need to gain their own experiences first-hand, they must go through the process and decide what reality is and what is just textbook drivel. It was doing exactly this that has allowed me to understand that there is a larger reality to the one we are conditioned to believe in. We are selling ourselves short by 'thinking' that reality is this physical dull, mundane existence we see broadcasted over our news channels or through social media. Trust me, there is something much larger and magical than you could even imagine, and the best thing, it's accessible to us all if we put the time and effort in.

Ryan Cropper - search him out on YouTube - is a young guy from England who has been having and inducing OBEs since a young age. He had a near death experience when younger which showed him that he had been popping in and out of his physical shell for a long time. There was much that he had forgotten about; this is something that may have happened to you and I, and we just do not recall it. He teaches people over YouTube how to have an OBE and to Astral Project one's consciousness while the body rests. He tells us:

1. Get comfortable by lying down on your back, focus on your breathing.

Invoke your imagination, with your eyes closed, and see yourself in first person walking around your room. Feel, smell and soak your senses with imagined stimuli.

Make an intention to notice your body falling asleep, your body and not your awareness. Will it fully, this is the power of intention.

Observation, you bear witness. If you are in the proper state, you should after some time feel an intense vibration within, possible whooshing sounds and sleep paralysis. (Do not fear this)

When the above stopped, just intend yourself to get up, stand up! Your essence will get and not your physical shell.

You may need to practice the above a few times before you succeed, but be mindful that when you do succeed the experience may only last a few shorts seconds too, until you become familiar with this state. Stick with it, however. Now, if you struggle still with the above practice, you may need to use Binaural Beats - as I mentioned in my experience - which are audio files that take your brainwaves down to a particular frequency that will induce sleep state with a cue to help your consciousness stay alerted without falling asleep entirely. You can get these audio files for free online, perhaps even utilising YouTube's extensive collections.

This is a perfect time to pick back up on the gentleman I mentioned while speaking about the fantastic Tom Campell and his work with consciousness. Bob Munroe was a radio broadcast executive who was well known for his research into altered states of consciousness and the founding of the aforementioned Monroe Institute. His 1971 book named 'Journeys Out of the Body' is fully credited with popularising the term we use today "out-of-body experience" or OBE (Some use OOBE). So how did it all start for this wealthy individual?

While experimenting with sleep-learning in 1950's, Bob Monroe experienced an unusual phenomenon, which he described as sensations of paralysis and vibration accompanied by a bright light that appeared to be shining on him from a shallow angle. Sounds familiar to my experiences above thus far and to what Ryan Cropper tells us, however, Bob induced this by accident, this was spontaneous! This occurred another nine times for Bob over the next six weeks, culminating in his first OBE. Bob recorded his account in his book, and went on to become a prominent researcher in the field of human consciousness. It was not as cut and dried as having the experiences and then writing about it, however. Bob was wealthy in his own right; he did not need to build laboratories or write books, the former costing him some of his wealth.

So why did he do this? Well, Bob thought there was something wrong with him, he at one point thought he was dying. This is rather simple to see why, especially if you have experienced these altered states we enter while taking part in the process. I recall Bob – on video – explaining that first time when he was floating near his bedroom ceiling while his wife lay sleeping below. He thought he had fallen onto the floor; his nose pushed against something, and wondered what the fountain emanating from the floor was. On closer inspection, he realised it was his light chandelier, so he spun around to see the bed, his wife and a gentleman lying next to her. Highly confused, he tried to see who this man was, then it became clear, it was him!

Bob panicked and began trying to swim through the air to get back into his body; fear gripped him as he thought he was dead or dying, and then suddenly he woke up in his body, sitting up in a sweat. This would begin the process of Bob Munroe seeking to find out what these experiences were - was he going crazy or was he gravely ill? He spoke to many friends in the field of psychology and medical doctors, only to be told he was healthy and nothing was wrong with him. How frustrating for Bob, he was having these otherworldly experiences and needed to find out how and why. He needed to study this and was prepared to sink some of his own wealth into finding out what was going on.

Perhaps Bob required proof he was not going crazy, to show his friends and family that there was science behind this and he had stumbled on something so fantastic, that the world must know about it. Remember this was the late 1950's, and unlike today, this type of phenomenon was not accepted in the slightest.   This is when Tom Campbell and the other scientists were invited to Bob's place to discuss the above. If Bob showed Tom how to do this, Tom would help Bob build that Lab and research this thoroughly with science. The rest, as they say, is history.

Surveys conducted in the past suggest that up to twenty percent of people claim to have had an Outer Body Experience at some point in their lives, the sensation of their consciousness, or spirit, leaving the physical body. This area shows us that in addition to consciousness being fundamental, consciousness can also operate outside of the body. Our awareness can detach and make choices using free will.

What if it could do this while the body was clinically dead? Would this then show us that consciousness was not the result of brain activity? Would show us that the afterlife we seek to communicate with is other individual units of consciousness, like us, that are operating without a physical shell in this reality we find ourselves within? Well, let me introduce you to Near Death Experiences, which show just this.

3. Near Death Experience (NDE)

An awareness of being dead, emotions that are positive, out of body experience, moving through a tunnel towards the light, communication with said light, meeting with deceased relatives and a having a life review – they are all common themes of what is a Near Death Experience (NDE). What is thought to be the oldest medical record of a NDE is a statement that was written in 1740 by French military physician Pierre-Jean du Monchaux. It may very well be the oldest such medical report, but for centuries, people have reported the other realm that exists outside the vibrations of this physical dimension.

We see it in religious scriptures, where people have taken them as literal meanings of everyday life, whereas the truth of the matter is that these were accounts of NDEs. Mainstream science has already dismissed the NDE , due to the fact that acceptance would cause the materialistic models to fall flat and cause a rethink of who we are and why we are here. Hardened sceptics have also attacked such experiences with a whole host of counter-explanations, ranging from lack of oxygen through to the lack of or excessive blood flow and the dying processes of a physical brain. These people avoid cases, where these explanations fall flat, as they do not fit into their hypothesis, and certainly bust their attempts to debunk the overwhelming evidence of life after physical death.

One such case was that of Pam Reynolds, a real eye-opener for my own research into the afterlife. Pam, from Atlanta, Georgia, was an American singer-songwriter. It was in 1991, at the young age of 35, that she shared the fact that she had a NDE during a brain operation performed by Robert F. Spetzler at the Barrow Neurological Institute in Phoenix, Arizona. Her case is, in fact, one of the most widely documented and cited NDEs due to the circumstances under which it occurred. Pam was under extremely close medical monitoring during the entire operation due to the complexity of the procedure. During the operation, she had no brain-wave activity and no blood flowing in her brain, which rendered her clinically dead.

She went on to claim several observations during the procedure, which later medical personnel reported to be accurate. When Pam's vital signs stopped, with the medical professionals satisfied that it was safe to begin, Neurosurgeon Robert F. Spetzler turned on his surgical saw and began to cut through Pam's skull. While this part of the surgery was taking place, Pam reported that she felt herself "pop" outside her body via her head and then hover above the operating table where her lifeless body lay. In this out of body state of awareness, she watched the doctors working on her lifeless body for a while. From her lofty position, she observed Dr Robert F. Spetzler sawing into her skull with what looked to her like an electric toothbrush.

Pam's awareness and senses were heightened in this state - she heard and reported later what the medical staff in the operating theatre had said and what would be proved to be precisely what was happening during the operation. At the time of this OBE state of awareness, every monitor attached to Pam's lifeless body registered no life. Pam could report precise words and medical terms used with which we can pinpoint within the surgery. This is a crucial point, as it's long been claimed by pseudo-sceptics - with no medical training or formal education in this field - that these types of experiences were at the beginning of the process while the body is not clinically dead.

We know in this case that an hour had elapsed with regards to the information relayed by Pam until she came back to the physical realm. It should have been physically impossible due to how deep she was under sedation - the clickers in her ears monitoring her state registered zero brain activity. This makes the Pam case extremely interesting and very difficult to debunk, which hardened sceptics and cynics still attempt, even at the level where their explanations go against the education and experience of the staff and neurosurgeon present.

Her experience did not stop here, however, as it was at this point that she began her ascent into what she deemed as a bright light. Pam's consciousness floated out of the operating theatre and travelled into the often mentioned tunnel, which had a light at the end of it. She reported that her deceased relatives and friends were waiting including her long-dead grandmother. She then met a favourite deceased uncle, who led her back to her body for her to re-enter it and come back to finish her challenges in life. Pam always compared the feeling of entering her dead body to "plunging into a pool of ice."

Here is Pam Reynolds' account of her NDE in her own words.

Pam Reynolds' NDE

The next thing I recall was the sound: It was a Natural "D." As I listened to the sound, I felt it was pulling me out of the top of my head. The further out of my body I got, the more clear the tone became. I had the impression it was like a road, a frequency that you go on ... I remember seeing several things in the operating room when I was looking down. It was the most aware that I think that I have ever been in my entire life ...I was metaphorically sitting on [the doctor's] shoulder. It was not like normal vision. It was brighter and more focused and clearer than normal vision ... There was so much in the operating room that I didn't recognize, and so many people.

I thought the way they had my head shaved was very peculiar. I expected them to take all of the hair, but they did not...

The saw-thing that I hated the sound of looked like an electric toothbrush and it had a dent in it, a groove at the top where the saw appeared to go into the handle, but it didn't ... And the saw had interchangeable blades, too, but these blades were in what looked like a socket wrench case ... I heard the saw crank up. I didn't see them use it on my head, but I think I heard it being used on something. It was humming at a relatively high pitch and then all of a sudden it went Brrrrrrrrr! like that.

Someone said something about my veins and arteries being very small. I believe it was a female voice and that it was Dr. Murray, but I'm not sure. She was the cardiologist. I remember thinking that I should have told her about that ... I remember the heart-lung machine. I didn't like the respirator ... I remember a lot of tools and instruments that I did not readily recognize.

There was a sensation like being pulled, but not against your will. I was going on my own accord because I wanted to go. I have different metaphors to try to explain this. It was like the Wizard of Oz - being taken up in a tornado vortex, only you're not spinning around like you've got vertigo. You're very focused and you have a place to go. The feeling was like going up in an elevator real fast.

And there was a sensation, but it wasn't a bodily, physical sensation. It was like a tunnel but it wasn't a tunnel.

At some point very early in the tunnel vortex I became aware of my grandmother calling me. But I didn't hear her call me with my ears ... It was a clearer hearing than with my ears. I trust that sense more than I trust my own ears.

The feeling was that she wanted me to come to her, so I continued with no fear down the shaft. It's a dark shaft that I went through, and at the very end there was this very little tiny pinpoint of light that kept getting bigger and bigger and bigger.

The light was incredibly bright, like sitting in the middle of a light bulb. It was so bright that I put my hands in front of my face fully expecting to see them and I could not. But I knew they were there. Not from a sense of touch. Again, it's terribly hard to explain, but I knew they were there ...

I noticed that as I began to discern different figures in the light - and they were all covered with light, they were light, and had light permeating all around them - they began to form shapes I could recognize and understand. I could see that one of them was my grandmother. I don't know if it was reality or a projection, but I would know my grandmother, the sound of her, anytime, anywhere.

Everyone I saw, looking back on it, fit perfectly into my understanding of what that person looked like at their best during their lives.

I recognized a lot of people. My uncle Gene was there. So was my great-great-Aunt Maggie, who was really a cousin. On Papa's side of the family, my grandfather was there ... They were specifically taking care of me, looking after me.

They would not permit me to go further ... It was communicated to me - that's the best way I know how to say it, because they didn't speak like I'm speaking - that if I went all the way into the light something would happen to me physically. They would be unable to put this me back into the body me, like I had gone too far and they couldn't reconnect. So they wouldn't let me go anywhere or do anything.

I wanted to go into the light, but I also wanted to come back. I had children to be reared. It was like watching a movie on fast-forward on your VCR: You get the general idea, but the individual freeze-frames are not slow enough to get detail.

Then they [deceased relatives] were feeding me. They were not doing this through my mouth, like with food, but they were nourishing me with something. The only way I know how to put it is something sparkly. Sparkles is the image that I get. I definitely recall the sensation of being nurtured and being fed and being made strong. I know it sounds funny, because obviously it wasn't a physical thing, but inside the experience, I felt physically strong, ready for whatever.

My grandmother didn't take me back through the tunnel, or even send me back or ask me to go. She just looked up at me. I expected to go with her, but it was communicated to me that she just didn't think she would do that. My uncle said he would do it. He's the one who took me back through the end of the tunnel. Everything was fine. I did want to go.

But then I got to the end of it and saw the thing, my body. I didn't want to get into it ... It looked terrible, like a train wreck. It looked like what it was: dead. I believe it was covered. It scared me and I didn't want to look at it.

It was communicated to me that it was like jumping into a swimming pool. No problem, just jump right into the swimming pool. I didn't want to, but I guess I was late or something because he [the uncle] pushed me. I felt a definite repelling and at the same time a pulling from the body. The body was pulling and the tunnel was pushing ... It was like diving into a pool of ice water ... It hurt!

When I came back, they were playing Hotel California and the line was "You can check out anytime you like, but you can never leave." I mentioned [later] to Dr. Brown that that was incredibly insensitive and he told me that I needed to sleep more. [laughter] When I regained consciousness, I was still on the respirator.

This NDE is considered by some to be concrete evidence of the survival of consciousness after death, and of a life after death. As mentioned above, key points were mentioned, such as the time frame of specific medical notifications from staff such as the thinning veins. The electric toothbrush visualisation recalled by Pam was, in fact, the saw for cutting the skull open. It has been verified and stated continuously by the staff that at no time was this visible to the patient. This includes before and after the surgery.

Robert F. Spetzler, the Neurosurgeon, played a key role in the telling of this experience, where he confirmed and acknowledged all of Pam's story as fact and impossible for her to recall or know at all. He, of course, stops short of claiming any survival of death but does acknowledge this is a highly unexplained case of intrigue. Speaking of Neurosurgeons, who are, if we are honest, the best placed people to describe the processes of the brain and the physical attributes to be expected. There is one who experienced first-hand the process of an NDE.

First, to put it into perspective, the process by which someone trains to become a neurosurgeon can take 14 years or longer. Wiki Professional tells us:

"The steps in the progression include four years of studying as an undergraduate and earning a bachelor's degree. Next, prospective neurosurgeons will need to apply to and get accepted into medical school which will take another four years. The last portion of the process is a six-year residency program."

The reason I highlight this before we go on to the case of Dr Eben Alexander, is that we actually have sceptical organisations with zero training in this field, apart from little more than access to other sceptics, books, message boards and good old Google and Wikipedia. They feel that these sources have all the information they require to debunk the unexplained. This may be so in cases where fraud does take place, or where there are other explanations. However, it does not work on professionals who have spent a significant portion of their lives in deep life or death study. So, when someone like Dr Eben Alexander tells us there is life after death, and he has seen it, we should sit up and listen carefully.

Dr. Eben Alexander spent over 25 years as an academic neurosurgeon, including 15 years at the Brigham & Women's

Hospital, the Children's Hospital and Harvard Medical School in Boston. Over those years, he dealt with hundreds of patients suffering from severe alterations in their level of consciousness. Many of those patients were rendered comatose by trauma, brain tumours, ruptured aneurysms, infections, or stroke. He thought he had an excellent idea of how the brain generates consciousness. I'm sure if you asked Dr Alexander about consciousness and the brain, much like most mainstream scientists or neurosurgeons - although this is changing fast - he would have told you that it was all a result of brain activity.

In other words, matter is fundamental, and awareness is a result of materialistic processes. It would take a brush with death through severe illness to show Dr Alexander that he was so much more than his body and send him on a quest to notify the world of this. He reports that in the predawn hours of November 10, 2008, he was driven into coma by a rare and mysterious bacterial Meningoencephalitis. He spent the following week in coma and on a ventilator, his prospects for survival were diminishing rapidly, and his brain was turning to mush. On the seventh day, to the surprise of everyone at the hospital, he started to awaken.

His memories of his life – or at least his access to these memories – had completely vanished inside of the coma. Yet, somehow, he awoke with memories of a fantastic deep realm that he had just adventured within. He even states that it's more real than this earthly one! His son advised him to write down everything he could remember about his adventure in the afterlife realms, specifically before he read anything about near-death experiences, physics or cosmology.

Some weeks later, he completed his initial recording of his remarkable journey, totalling over 20,000 words in length. Then he started reading, and was astonished by the commonalities between his journey and that of so many others reported throughout all cultures, continents and millennia. His experience clearly revealed that we are conscious in spite of our brain – that, in fact, consciousness is at the root of all existence. Dr Eben Alexander written books about his experiences and his new thought processes. He was brave enough to speak out about it, regardless of his past life as a sceptical medical professional. I highly recommend his book, *Proof of Heaven, A Neurosurgeon's Journey into the Afterlife*.

With so many great examples of our consciousness surviving physical death or brain-eating infections that are miraculously cured and go against the grain of materialistic science, the question is, why do we not hear more about this? We can only speculate about the why's, whether it is a lack of funding, as no gain can be made by those holding the purse strings, or perhaps a reluctance to rip up the rigid theories of mainstream science. Mainstream media does cover some stories, but always it seems to come across as a quirky, wacky world story to be giggled at or recorded onto the end of the more important negative news in the world as light relief.

Nevertheless, such reports of NDE's go back in time, predating the aforementioned medical reports and embedded into scriptures and writings from times long gone. It does not matter which race, culture or religion involved; the experiences are all vastly similar. They mimic OBE's, which in turn opens up possibilities to experience these realms - as I have - without needing to die or nearly die. Our consciousness does not need the physical body to be active nor even alive in all honesty. Our awareness carries on, which then begins to open up the possibility of finding other such units of consciousness that we term as spirits, ghosts and the like.

Researching the Unseen

4. Types Of Afterlife Activity

Sentient & Non-Sentient Apparitions.

It is understandable that an air of confusion engulfs the average person when terminology and phrases are discussed, those obscure buzz words that are often shared between teams, researchers and enthusiasts alike. How can the ordinary person on the street understand what is transpiring without a more open discussion and thorough explanations? I wish to point out the difference between a sentient haunting and a non-sentient haunting, and I can only imagine that thus far you are scratching your head wondering what on earth this means, and what the implications are.

Sentient means a life form with the ability to feel, and perceive things along with conscious interaction. The non-sentient is, of course, the opposite to this, and in a moment I will explain in what context this can apply to an alleged haunting. In my time working within the field of paranormal research, I have amassed a vast amount of knowledge, personally hypothesised and partaken in great lengthy discussions about this topic. Many hours have been, and are still, spent in deep brainstorming sessions with very able investigators such as Christopher Huff from the North-East of England. We dig deep and come to some temporarily satisfactory conclusions, in how we would define the above.

Setting the Scene

Imagine the scene; you are in the kitchen washing your dishes when suddenly, a full manifestation of a transparent ghostly figure catches your eye. On noticing this manifestation you lock eyes with it, it smiles at you, moves a few objects in your environment with resulting sounds, and then dissipates into the ether. You call out for the phantom to make noise again if it's real; it obliges with tapping on demand, as if in some advanced communication with you. You have just witnessed a sentient apparition, where the manifestation has consciously interacted with you.

Interaction is the key ingredient here, whether this is with you or with the environment you and the apparition are operating within. Sentient apparitions are points of consciousness much like ourselves but without the physical body. This sort of intelligence is able to interact with us. The apparition may be haunting the location due to some deep bond emotionally with the property or someone who lives there.

However, the apparition might also just be visiting, and is is not active 24/7 in the location. Reasons for visitation may vary from a connection to the owners, management or staff, through to knowing that a certain individual was going to be present at a given moment. This is the type of haunting that can produce Actual Voice Phenomena (AVP) or manipulate sound waves and electronics that are set up to induce communication.

Scene Number Two

Using the same circumstances, again washing the dishes, this time you catch a glimpse of the phantom from the corner of your eye, and then attempt to lock eye contact - the apparition completely ignores you, with no interaction at all, and it seems as if it's following a set movement pattern. There is no awareness from this manifestation, and on top of this, it's been reported doing the same movements without interaction by many past witnesses.

This is a non-sentient haunting, a recording if you like, which has somehow etched its energy into the environment and is triggered under certain circumstances. Now, to attempt to call out for a sign from a non-sentient apparition is akin to asking your coffee table to make a noise if it can hear you. It's utterly pointless and a waste of time and energy. Many locations with a reported activity may be subject to this. Thus, we gather no real usable evidence. Some researchers may even class the place as not haunted, when the better definition would be a residual haunting, with a non-sentient energy being active.

Non-sentient apparitions are rife; you will find a plethora of reports of them if you look through online witness reports. Some of the more common ones involve marching soldiers near old battlefields, who seem to walk a particular path and at times on old roads that are long gone. Other reports may highlight an emotional event replayed time and time again. Perhaps a disaster such as a train crash where we see the train head towards its demise. This is pure energy, projecting into our environment for the conscious observers. Only good prior research and some investigative skills would allow the proper definition to be used.

We certainly would not want to waste time using audio communication experimentation in the hope of gaining a capture from a non-sentient apparition. It's only when we get a clear response, good witness testimony of interaction, and physical movement of objects, that we begin to dig deep and apply the proper protocols for spirit communication. Some in the field do this; some do not even know the difference, unfortunately.

We could hypothesise at great length into the how, why and what of non-sentient energy and triggers, but experience tells me it could get lengthy and messy. Let's just say it's an area I am still looking at, along many other able investigators. So to you, the wonderful readers and fellow researchers, think about your experiences and have a look at what group your story may fall under. This is the first step to understanding the circumstances surrounding what you have personally experienced – or in some cases – may be researching.

How can you adapt your sessions, gather evidence, or trigger more activity? Jump outside the box and think differently on this topic.

So to recap:

•   Sentient – Interaction and physical manipulation.
Non-Sentient – No Interaction and Identical Sighting Circumstances

Crisis & Deathbed Apparitions

There can be nothing more shocking for a person than seeing the apparition of a loved one visit you as they pass elsewhere in the world. Usually as solid as you and I, the loved one will visit to say goodbye before they continue their journey into the afterlife. a short period of time, the phone will ring, the witness already awaiting their news, as it's confirmed the loved one has passed over. It brings shock, sadness and also comfort to us all. Let's look at some examples of such events:

Little Annie & Visitations

There was this lady (we'll call her Annie) that was a friend of my mom's, and I lived with her for a few months after college.

I worked 2nd shift, so I was up late watching TV after everyone else was in bed. Annie comes walking into the living room, half asleep. I say, "What's going on, Annie?" and she says, "My grandmother just called."

I'm like, "Nooooo, no one has called."

She insists that she just talked to her grandmother and that her grandmother called to tell her goodbye and now she wants to call her family to check on her.

"Nonsense," I say. "It was just a dream. Don't bother your family in the middle of the night. Go back to bed and call them in the morning." And she goes back to bed.

About an hour later, I'm just getting into bed when the phone rings. No, shit. And it's her family calling to tell her that her grandmother died about an hour ago.

The grandmother was old, but not sick or on death's bed or anything. Annie did not remember any of this the next day, and we never spoke of it. I thought about this for years and struggled with labelling it a ghost story or just an eerie coincidence. My sceptical and logical tendencies decided to label it a coincidence. The only times I have re-told this story have been to people who do not know Annie in situations where everyone is telling their "ghost-stories."

THEN

About a decade later, Annie died unexpectedly. I went to her funeral, and her brother delivered a eulogy. In it, he tells this story.

When Annie was about 4, her great-grandmother died. All the family was gathered in the house, and someone noticed that little Annie had disappeared. After a brief search, they found her in a bedroom, rolling on the floor laughing.

"What on earth are you laughing about, Annie?" and little Annie replies, "Great-grandma was tickling me. She came to tell me goodbye."

– Posted by Hoodooz39; Reddit

Children do appear to be more prone to such visitations, as highlighted in the above story about 'Annie' and her grandmother. We can hypothesise that this is due to children being less conditioned at a younger age. The mere mention of such sightings, in most cases, would have parents and teachers proclaiming that an overactive imagination is at play.

I beg to differ on the above; I feel such gifts are conditioned out of us as we are led to conform to a more material existence to fit into our cultural norms. However, it's not just younger children who report crisis apparitions; age is no limitation, a spirit may appear for the final time to comfort all ages in their family.

He Waved One Last Time

I was fourteen years old, a freshman in high school and had just torn the cartilage in my knee playing football and had big knee support on my leg.

My grandfather was sick in Florida, and we had flown into to see him. He was bedridden with a live-in nurse. Everyone knew it was the end. One night we went to dinner at my great-aunt's house, and I couldn't sit at the table because of the knee support (it didn't bend). So, I'm sitting next to the table with everyone else, facing the outside window.

Looking out the window, I see my grandfather looking in, just briefly, small wave and he was gone. AND he didn't look like he had earlier in the day, emaciated and yellow from cancer. He looked like I would always remember him. It freaked me the fark out. I just sat there for a few seconds stunned. Then I turned to my mother and her sisters and told them that grandpa must have died, she asked why I said that and I told her what I had just seen.

Then the phone rang, and it was my grandfather's nurse, he had just died like five minutes prior. Now, everybody was freaked the fark out.

– Posted by Release the Hounds; Fark

There's never any drama to these visitations; they are just a way to say goodbye and that all is well. They are extremely common, and I could share story after story submitted to me or within the public domain. Such is the number of experiences had, that we could easily write a whole new book on crisis apparitions alone. Let's share one final experience before we move on to talk about other types of an apparition. This one, rather than visiting, was still active after passing into the non-physical.

Science Teacher's Apparition

I was driving home from work at about 4:00 in the afternoon. Stopping at a stop sign, I saw my high school biology teacher walking down the street (I was at a complete stop, and there was no mistaking who it was).

I honked my horn and waved towards him; It took a moment for him to recognise me, then he smiled and waved back. Then he continued walking.

My dad got a phone call at about 9:00 that evening (my dad was a teacher at my high school). Mr Hume had died in his home of a heart attack that morning around 11:00 a.m.

– Posted by flaggboy42; Fark

Crisis apparitions usually move on into the afterlife and have very little to do with actual hauntings. It's going to be extremely rare to make communication with such entities, as the presence is only meant for the conscious observer, who have the only link. This is not to say we cannot still communicate with our loved ones. Apure intention to make communication and an observing for the subtle reply may be all that is in order. One energy that we would prefer not to call out for would be the mischievous spirit, however, the extremely active and noisy energy that has been classified as a poltergeist.

Poltergeist Type Phenomena

You've seen the movies right? Perhaps heard of the massive cases such as the Enfield Poltergeist happenings? This type of activity can be rather alarming due to the events that occur, I mean, there is no mistaking that something out of the ordinary is happening when you come face to face with a poltergeist. Poltergeist is German for noisy ghost or noisy spirit, mainly due to the characteristics of reported cases dating back to the 1st century.

We are talking about some serious physical activity in the form of objects being moved, levitation, punching, biting and scratching to name but a few. To the casual observer, this is utterly astonishing in the extreme, a real world view changer. They have traditionally been described as some type of troublesome entity, mainly due to the severe physical occurrences. Regardless of culture, the levels of activity always seem to follow a particular pattern.

I've seen reports from Europe, USA, Australia, Japan, Philippines, Brazil and India. I'm sure there is much more out with my knowledge will be in the literature too. Is it really a spirit or ghost, however? Like many subjects under the paranormal banner, we must hypothesise due to the lack of ability to understand every facet of what we see reported or personally experience.

I have long surmised that poltergeist type activity is related to the person and not the location of activity. This was reached by looking at many cases where a common theme would present itself to me. Mostly, I would see that activity was centred around prepubescent children - mainly girls - who were moving into their adolescent years and that for some strange reason, this attracted the activity.

Could telekinesis also be at play here, could the mix of energies within the child be causing such at a deep subconscious level? We must rule nothing out of course! Nevertheless, we have a plethora of cases which are famous and shining an intense light upon such phenomena.

The "Mackie poltergeist"

According to a pamphlet first published by local minister Alexander Telfair in 1696, a farm called The Ring-Croft of Stocking inhabited by the family was subject to poltergeist activity.

Stone mason - and farmer - Andrew Mackie was witness to mysterious occurrences such as stones throwing, the moving of cattle, buildings set on fire, strange voices heard, family members allegedly beat/dragged, and strange notes found written in what appeared to be blood.

Telfair wrote that rocks seemingly hit neighbours and staves beat them. They also reported that they felt a ghostly arm, which quickly vanished. In the pamphlet, Telfair described things he had considered "to have been the occasion of the Trouble", including: MacKie supposedly taking an oath to devote his first child to the Devil; clothes left in the house by a "woman of ill repute; and failure to burn a tooth buried under the threshold stone by a previous tenant advised by a spey-wife.

According to the story, after Telfair and several other clergymen said prayers at the farm, the trouble eventually subsided. Sacheverell Sitwell in his book *Poltergeists* (1940) wrote that events described in the story fabricated by one of Mackie's children using ventriloquism. Sitwell observes that a voice awoke MacKie, telling him he would "be troubled till Tuesday" and that if Scotland did not "repent" it would "trouble every family in the land". According to Sitwell, "Here, again there can be no doubt whatever that the actual Poltergeist was one of the children of the family. It had, in fact, learnt to ventriloquize. This, though, does not make the mystery any less unpleasant".

Ring-Croft of Stocking, described as "a smallholding on the top side of Auchencairn", was located in the parish of Rerrick, now part Dumfries and Galloway. Reportedly, a dead tree is all that remains of the MacKie farm today. We tend not to go looking for poltergeist type phenomena when exploring allegedly haunted locations. Mostly due to the ideas that it's a person centred activity and not one of a particular area.

The only time I've been called into such cases, was when asked to by the owners of a private house due to their fear levels. In the small town of Cowdenbeath, in Fife, I would face one such case. The owners fled the building, positioned on the high street above shops, and left a lot of their belongings behind. I took, and coordinated, a team of researchers to look at the building. We extensively tested the environment and attempted a whole manner of communication techniques but were to be left disappointed. Perhaps the activity had ceased altogether, or maybe the energy was centred around the children as mentioned previously. We never got a final answer to that one.

5. A-Z of Paranormal Definitions

Terminology can vary slightly depending on whom you speak with or which articles you may read. The beautiful thing about paranormal research and observations is that there are so many approaches and viewpoints. This is healthy, yet it should also be remembered that no one, including scientists or psychics, have all the answers. This is why it's better to approach from your own flexible viewpoint.

I may regularly use terms that the public is not familiar with, this has prompted the placement of this following inclusion to assist you the reader.

A
Afterlife
Life after our physical body ceases to be; it is speculated that we move into another realm or dimension in an energy type form if we can call it such.

Anomaly
A deviation from common rule or condition, an unexplainable happening, most commonly referred to paranormal activity and the material collected.

Apparition
Supernatural appearance of a person or thing, especially a ghost; a spectre or phantom that may be translucent or solid. More commonly associated with a deceased personal visiting [Sentient] or a recorded replay [Non-Sentient]

Apport
The production of objects by apparently supernatural means at a spiritualists' séance or within a haunted location or area experiencing such phenomena.

Astral Travel
Astral Travel (or Astral Projection) is an interpretation of out-of-body experience (OBE) that assumes the existence of an "astral

body" separate from the physical body and capable of travelling outside it.

Astral projection or travel denotes the astral body leaving the physical body to move in other realms.

Aura
The unique atmosphere/energy or quality that seems to surround and be generated by a person, thing, or place. Some say they can see auras; they are therefore able to tell a person's mood or current health status, some even able to help repair with the acceptance of the participant.

Automatic Writing
Writing said to be produced by a spiritual, occult, or subconscious agency rather than by the conscious intention of the writer.

Automatism
The performance of actions without conscious thought or intention, such as an Ouija Board, automatic writing [see above], or pendulum swinging.

B
Banshee
(Irish folklore) a female spirit who wails to warn of impending death.

Being
The state or quality of having existence, a living being.

Belief
Something one accepts as true or real; a firmly held opinion or conviction. Sceptics have strong views much in the identical case of religious people or spiritualists do

Benign Spirit
A spirit that is not harmful [see **Malevolent Spirit**]

Bi-location

Being (or appearing to be) in two different places at the same time. A remote viewing term that means consciousness is fully at the target. The target can be a person, place, event, or object.

C
Channelling
The act or practice of serving as a medium through which a spirit guide purportedly communicates with living persons.

Clairgustance
Means clear tasting – a psychic ability which enables someone experience a sense of taste with no apparent physical stimulus.

Clairvoyant
Someone with the psychic ability to see events or people, which have not occurred yet.

An individual who claims to have a supernatural ability to perceive events in the future or beyond normal sensory contact.

Can contact the deceased through vibrational work if such spirit is in the vicinity and wishing to do so.

Clairaudient
The psychic ability to hear voices and sounds that are inaudible to the normal human ear.

The supposed power to hear things outside the range of normal perception. [clair(voyance) + audience.]

Clairsentient
The psychic ability to feel things that are not commonly perceived by most people. The psychic ability of clairsentience literally means clear sensing.

Cleansing
The act of formally and ritualistically purification of an area. To rid a person, place, or thing of something seen as unpleasant, unwanted, or defiling.

Cold Spot
An area where the temperature is lower than the surrounding environment. Cold spots are believed to be created when a ghost is present within that area. As an example, while researching within Huntingtower Castle, a cold spot was sourced in one of the rooms. Likened to walking past an open freezer with no natural source. Can be measured on the equipment.

Collective Apparition
An apparition seen by several people at the same time.

Continuance
Commonly referred to as the survival of the soul after mortal death, the state of remaining in existence or operation.

Crisis Apparition
These are apparitions of the dying or recently dead. This is the most often reported apparition. Many such examples exist and a widespread phenomenon.

Curse
An appeal or prayer for evil or misfortune to befall someone or something as well as the after effect on the desired target. Using intent to curse another, who unknowingly may be affected. Rife within some African villages.

D
Deja`Vu
The experience of thinking that a new situation had occurred before, an ability to know what is coming next.

Widespread phenomena and not explained adequately by science nor cynics.

Dematerialization
The fading or disappearance of a physical object or apparition.

Discarnate

A spirit that exists without a physical body. Not having a physical body.

Discernment
The ability to feel or perceive something with the use the mind and the senses. Capacity to judge well.

Disembodied
Separated from or existing without the body. Lacking any obvious physical source, ie a sound, like footsteps.

Disembodied Voice
A voice that is heard that comes from no physical body, also known as EVP or also can be heard without the assistance of recording devices. [See Mary Kings Close – EVP]

Divination
The practice of seeking knowledge of the future or the unknown by supernatural means.

Doppelganger
German for "Double-goer" A person's duplicate or identical counterpart, [see bi-location or astral travel] also a ghostly double of a living person that haunts its living counterpart.

E
Ectoplasm
A substance resulting from spirit materialisation, channelling, and telekinesis. A viscous substance supposed to exude from the body of a medium during a spiritualistic trance and to form the material for the manifestation of Spirit.

Electromagnetic Field (EMF)
An electric and magnetic energy that radiates from radio and light waves to gamma and cosmic rays.

Some speculate that spirit can use this to manifest or interact with our reality.

This continues to be an unknown within the field and all too easily dismissed or accepted without further study and experimentation.

It should be noted, EMF Detectors are not "Ghost Detectors".

Electronic Voice Phenomena (EVP)
The recording of noises (usually voices) which is out of the range of human hearing.

The main principle behind this phenomenon is that electronic microphones do not discriminate against sound fields, the way human ears do.

In effect, it will record all noises and funnel them into our normal hearing range; this allows the researcher to review such and report findings.

EMF Detector
A device that measures and detects changes in the electromagnetic field and not locate ghosts.

Entity
A being or self-contained bodiless form of existence, most commonly referred to as ghost or spirit. Can manifest or remain unseen awhile causing other phenomena.

Extrasensory Perception
 (ESP) The faculty of perceiving things by means other than the known senses, e.g., by telepathy or clairvoyance.

F
False Positive
Any evidence indicating an affirmative result when in fact all conditions are normal. Can be caused by equipment malfunction or misinterpretation of the data obtained. Strong belief systems and intent are also being explored as possibilities for unique data, for example, the double slit experiment in quantum physics.

G
Gauss Meter

A device that is used to measure the electromagnetic field also referred to as EMF detectors or magnetometers.

Ghost
An apparition of a dead person that is believed to appear or become manifest to the living, typically as a nebulous image. Usually referred to as a Non-Sentient.

Ghosting
The appearance of false anomalies caused by bleed over on a video surveillance set up caused by bad grounding or shielding.

H
Haunted
A person, place or an object to which a spirit is attached. The spirits can be human or inhuman in nature. For example of a place said to be frequented by a ghost: "It looked like a classic haunted mansion."

Haunting
The presence of a spirit, non-sentient or entity, as associated with one or more persons, places, or objects.

The haunting can be an actual sentient communicative entity/spirit or may, in fact, be a recorded energy that has somehow etched itself into our environment, replaying in the correct conditions.

I
Ideomotor effect
A psychological phenomenon wherein a subject makes motions unconsciously (i.e., without conscious awareness). As in reflexive responses to pain, the body sometimes reacts reflexively to ideas alone without the person consciously deciding to take action. For instance, tears are produced by the body unconsciously in reaction to the emotion of sadness, usually without any intervention of conscious will.

Incubus
A male demon believed to have sexual intercourse with sleeping women.

Usually teamed with sleep paralysis or similar type effects.

Intuition
The ability to understand something immediately, without the need for conscious reasoning.

A thing that one knows or considers likely from instinctive feeling e.g., from sight, taste, feel, smell, or hearing rather than conscious reasoning.

May emanate from our right hemisphere rather than the left hemisphere.

Invocation
The summoning of a deity or the supernatural.

K
Karma
Term used in Hinduism and Buddhism. The sum of a person's actions in this and previous states of existence viewed as deciding their fate, Destiny or fate, following as effect from cause.

Kirlian Photography
A technique for recording photographic images of corona discharges and hence, supposedly, the auras of living creatures.

L
Lens flare
The light scattered in lens systems through generally unwanted image formation mechanisms, such as internal reflection and scattering from material inhomogeneities in the lens.

Levitation
A phenomenon sometimes encountered in hauntings, particularly with a poltergeist, rare yet credibly reported, where solid objects (including persons) are moved and lifted by an unseen force. The first historically documented occurrence was that of St. Francis of Assisi in the 14th century.

Ley lines

Ley lines are alleged alignments of many places of geographical interest, such as ancient monuments and megaliths. Some suggest the possibility of paranormal activity emanating near these areas due to earth energies, much like human energies, with the ability to evoke manifestations and such.

Lore
A body of traditions and knowledge on a subject or held by a particular group typically passed from person to person by word of mouth.

M
Malevolent Spirit
A spirit with a destructive behaviour or harmful intentions. These spirits will destroy or damage things of a personal or financial value for the sake of hurting others. [See also **Benevolent Spirit**]

Manifestation
An event, action, or object that shows or embodies something, appearance or taking of form of an entity.

The appearance of an apparition, the action or fact of showing.

Materialization
[As Above] The sudden appearance of a spirit, apparition, or ghost.

Matrixing
[See **Pareidolia**]

Medium
A person that acts as a bridge between the living and the dead. [See **Clairvoyant**]

Metaphysics
Said to have been instituted by Aristotle, the line of philosophical thought which seeks the "why and wherefore". The study of which is beyond and above the laws of physics. The non-physical,

N
Near-Death Experience (NDE)

Experiences of people after they have been pronounced clinically dead, or been very close to death.

Energy body allegedly moves into the afterlife, to be met with relatives, other energy beings who take on the form you are most comfortable with whether religious or a loved one.

This is said to be done in order to place you at ease in the transition.

Many return to tell of their experience and change their life accordingly afterwards.

Cannot be explained by science and will not be tolerated by pseudo-sceptics due to their materialistic viewpoint and belief system.

Necromancy
The practice of communicating with the dead to obtain knowledge of the future, others' secrets, etc. An archaic term, the necromancer was said to employ magic spells and conjuration to summon, then banish, the spirits of the dead.

Still practised heavily even in this day and age by many members of society and those in the know.

Rituals often accompany such contacts and traditions.

Non-Sentient
An apparition that does not interact during manifestation.

Usually, replays a certain past event with high emotional significance, left over energy with no means of interaction and hypothetically fades with time.

The trigger for such replays can be anything from environmental conditions to the witness' emotional state of being.

O
Orb
A spherical imperfection that appears in a picture or video. Usually translucent or semi-transparent in density, and usually white (or white-ish) in colour.

There has been no conclusive evidence that orbs are spirits or ghosts.

However, common causes for orbs include (but aren't limited to) dust, rain/moisture/snow, insects, camera malfunctions, infra-red light sources, light reflections, lasers, reflectors, smoke, flying particles, and cracked or dirty lenses.

Real time witnessing of such has been reported, where no recording device is used, and the phenomena are seen by naked eye.

Ruling out ball lightning, we may then get closer to a paranormal origin. Usually, photographs with such are treated with scepticism due to the testing done by some and resulting in natural causes outweighing paranormal possibilities.

Ouija Board
A game board that some believe is capable of communicating with spirits.

P
Pareidolia
Referenced in 1994 by Steven Goldstein, describes a psychological phenomenon involving a vague and random stimulus (often an image or sound) being perceived as significant.

The human mind's desire to relate unfamiliar object, condition, or image to a familiar object, condition, or image.

Example: Seeing shapes in clouds. The human eye desires to see things it is familiar with, even if it has to create them. This is why most people see ghosts in perfectly ordinary pictures that just happen to coincidentally contain what appears to be a face or an apparition.

Granted, it might very well be an entity, but caution must be used to avoid perceptual association when investigating the paranormal.

Phantom
An apparition or a spectre. Ghost – spectre – apparition – wraith

Phenomena
Any occurrence that is observable or recorded that goes above and beyond the natural, aka, Para-normal in nature.

Poltergeist
German for "noisy ghost" *Polter* is German for "to crash about" and *Geist* means "Spirit".

This is a sporadic occurrence wherein random objects are moved and sounds produced by an unseen force, the sole purpose of which seems to be to draw attention to itself.

The phenomena always involve a particular individual, frequently adolescent.

My research suggests girls are more prone to this than boys; this then raises the questions about energy and why females have a greater deal to aid possible activity such as this.

Precognition
Foreknowledge of an event, esp. foreknowledge of a paranormal kind.

Psychic
Relating to the psyche, of the mind or soul, rather than the mundane. Psychic is the most familiar and bandied-about term encountered in paranormal research (a "psychic investigation", etc.). See also Clairvoyant

Q
Quantum Physics
The branch of physics based on quantum theory. An exciting new area with closer movement to answers about the nature of reality. Old school scientists are still trying to restrict this area much in the same way as ancient religions stifle forward spiritual movement.

R
Reincarnation

A person or animal in whom a particular soul is believed to have been reborn.

Remote Viewing

Remote viewing (RV) is the ability to gather information about a distant or unseen target using paranormal means

Residual Spirit

Believed to be a psychic imprint of a scene that keeps repeating itself. With this type of haunting no interaction with the spirit is known to occur. [See Non-Sentient]

S

Séance

A meeting of people to receive spiritualistic messages. Usually around a table and joining hands to raise vibrations and energy.

Shuck

A phantom black dog with glowing yellow eyes. Hikers in the British Isles who encounter this spectral creature by lonely roadsides and paths are said to be doomed to die within a year of the sighting. It is from this legend that Sir Arthur Conan Doyle drew his inspiration for his Sherlock Holmes adventure, "The Hound of the Baskervilles" (1902).

Sceptic

A person inclined to question or doubt all accepted opinions. Has a duty to stay open-minded and question everything and remain attached to no belief system while doing so.

This is opposite to Pseudo-Scepticism, whereas we have debunkers who make it their job to deny everything even without a proper investigation.

Examples of such are James Randi the illusionist and his band of merry men who hang on his words without independent thought and real critical thinking.

Proper examples would be: one who is yet undecided as to what is true; one who is looking or inquiring for what is true or an inquirer after facts or reasons.

Skeptical
See above, discount the Pseudo-Sceptical approach which harms real evolving in subjects and stifles advancements.

Sleep Paralysis
A state of seeming to be awake but unable to move, some report being unable to talk or shout and even seeing the old hag. Whether brain chemical or OBE, this is to be thoroughly investigated.

Spectre
A ghost or apparition.

Spirit
Existence apart from, or transcending, the purely physical; also, the life force of an organism. A spirit commonly refers to deceased and returning energy in its new form. The non-physical part of a person or animal that is the seat of emotions and character; the soul.

Spiritualism
A science, philosophy, and religion using the doctrine of metaphysics, belief in the continuity of life after death and communication with this life for the advancement of civilisation and personal growth.

Not limited to religious in any way.

Succubus
"Female" counterpart of the incubus, a demonic entity said to inspire lust in men, sometimes capable of physically attacking and inflicting injuries (bruises, slashes). Following a nocturnal visitation from a succubus, the human victim will always feel ill and depleted of vitality, and inexplicably "un-clean."

Synchronicity
An unexplained system of causal interaction, which binds together events, actions and thought, manifesting as uncanny coincidences.

Term for and the existence of this phenomenon was first proposed by the pioneering psychoanalyst, Carl Gustav Jung (a contemporary of Sigmund Freud). Synchronicity indicates there is more to the Universe than our understanding of simple cause and effect, and that the subtleties of the mind and matter are somehow interconnected.

This is a genuine phenomenon; everyone has encountered it at one time or another.

Thinking of someone- family and friends - and they call, bump into someone in the street after talking about them recently and other thought and event anomalies.

Bypasses mere coincidence.

T
Table-tipping
An experiment in psychokinesis, which can fairly easily be replicated by some. Three or four participants lightly place their fingers along the edges of a small table top, then in unison intend the table to move. With sufficient cooperation and concentration, and after several minutes of chanting, the table should start to wobble, pivot on its legs and even raid in the air. Whether the he power of the mind, subconscious moment or spiritual contact, the jury is out!

Telekinesis
A psychic phenomenon wherein objects are remotely displaced and moved around, solely by the powers of the mind.

Telepathy
The ability to communicate directly through mind-to-mind contact and to perceive information directly from another's mind, without resorting to the use of the five known senses.

W
White Noise

A hiss-like sound, formed by combining all audible frequencies. Used to aid spiritual contact via audible recoding devices.

Wraith/Wrayth
The image of a person appearing shortly before or after his or her death; the term can also be applied to a ghost.

Now that we are up to speed on the type of activity and the terminology used by various researchers, observers and enthusiasts, we can move onto the next chapter and talk about methods to employ

7. Methods For Afterlife Research

Equipment for the Search

In such a diverse field of research and observation, we have the opportunity for vast differences in methodologies. Equipment is an area of personal choice for each researcher, investigator or field observer. The emphasis is placed heavily on environmental monitoring and continuous recording while also taking in-depth notes. We are observers first and foremost, and then when the need arises, there is more than enough scope for full investigation and continued research.

To simplify, what we want to do is check for subtle changes in our immediate environment. To do this we will need to know what the temperature is, the electromagnetic field readings - AC for sure, DC if you have the correct meter for such - and the remaining part will be you and how you feel on the location.

Audio Equipment.

Forget photographs with illuminated particles (orbs) or film footage with dubious condensed breath – unless you can prove otherwise of course – and begin to look into the area of audio capture while attempting to collect paranormal activity on location. Anyone who follows my work in the field knows I prefer to test and advance with the Echovox audio application, Voxbox & ITC IP APP by Mark Coultous and Jonathan Garaways Scanning Box but even basic EVP techniques with any type of audio device capable of capture can be your number one friend.

Let me tell you why: I, like everyone else out there, cannot guarantee people will come into contact with an apparition or other likewise activity, but I can point you in a particular direction that may enhance the possibility. That direction happens to be the area of sound capture, and more importantly, possible voices caught on recording devices. If you ever work with me on a location, you will regularly hear me say that I feel substantial evidence will be gained through the area of sound, frequencies, and vibrational energy when we tackle the subject of afterlife communication.

I believe we are approaching the time where we can fully understand that those who are more developed regarding intuitive abilities and mediumistic communication are tapping into informational frequencies, much like a radio picking up the radio station that has been tuned in perfectly. I believe we can get access to the same informational frequencies via sound waves, and the manipulation of such by unseen energies that can move this data from the non-physical – where they are operating – into the physical through this mode of delivery.

Bear in mind, this is very similar to how a medium works, only we are accessing a more clairaudient area of working, rather than clairvoyant. We are also doing it via sound devices, carefully scanning, operating, and analysing certain signals that can be heard by anyone regardless of levels of ability or belief systems. I feel the more technology advances, the more we can tap into these areas by testing new techniques, and presenting them as circumstantial evidence. We may just go far enough to prove the existence of another bigger picture reality that we cannot see in this physical life. To put it simply, we can gain certain amounts of communication via sound – & phrases – that we can analyse and present as a part of the puzzle that we hope to solve.

This is where you come in: regardless of experience, anyone can start with a simple recording device and set it up in an area with reported activity. You can go further, purchase applications such as Echovox, Voxbox or ITC IP App by Coultous and begin full testing and reporting of the results you gain. All you need to start work in this area is the mind set to find the truth, the ability to create good questions to ask using the device – remembering to leave a gap for answers – and the patience to upload the results to your PC so you can analyse the recordings. The latter part is essential, as rarely do we hear results live, we must carefully listen back, slow down, and pay attention to the recordings when done. I promise if you do this, you will increase the results to an astonishing level. If you skip this part, you will be left underwhelmed.

I firmly stick by my initial assertions when I say that the breakthrough in afterlife communication that everyone can get access to and understand, will come in the form of sound. It's gained through some type of hypothetical manipulation of sound waves by the unseen energies that at times impact upon our world. The excellent news is, you can be part of this by beginning to test, explore, and openly probe this exciting area of paranormal research and observational work.

What do I need?

- Sound recording device: This can be a Dictaphone or even a Smartphone (put it into Aeroplane mode)

Echovox/Voxbox/ITC IP Application: Optional, but as I will explain next, will elevate your amount of captures gained in real time.

Questions of Relevance: Research the location you plan to visit online for location history and names of personalities

Access to Haunted Location: There are a ton of free ones, or you may wish to join a group or event to test your thoughts (and equipment)

Audacity or Adobe Audition: One is free and one if not, both can do the same thing, however. You may be able to source a free Adobe earlier edition as they do at times give these away. These will be your sound analysis programs.

Open Flexible Mind & Burning Desire: Very much overlooked this one; we will talk more about this later. Clear your mind, remain open to everything, yet attached to no outcomes.

What Is Echovox or Voxbox?

What we have here is a fantastic piece of software that can run on your Smartphone or PC tablet [I use the Android Version] and can then be discreetly used on location. You see, the hypothesis here – and as I've continued to present openly for years now – is the unique ability of this system to provide coherent local dialect captures using sound-waves, frequencies and produce an electronic soup of potentiality.

The software seems to tap into those areas that spiritual mediums can, albeit, without the visual aspect or symbolic jigsaw building that many of these gifted people experience. This experiment software is purely sound you see, with audio phoneme sound banks playing at high randomness. This then begins to allow non-physical energies to use these non-physical fields we are creating, utilising in the unique creation of turning audio chaos into coherent order.

Does It Work?

I have embarked on a study that's lasted more than four years. So it's early days thus far, but I will say, I'm impressed, and I can assure people this is not a gimmicky piece of software or one of these phone apps for fun. You see, I too was sceptical, to begin with, and needed to see, or in the case of the application hear something, before I would undertake serious study into this area of my research. I would certainly be wasting no money on gimmicks or my precious time looking into something that did not make hypothetical sense to my already flexible formed ideas.

How Do I Get Results?

If you have a pre-set judgement of "This will not work", guess what - the chances of it working are limited. It's been proven over and over that the very act of thinking is measurable outside the head – in the form of frequency – meaning what you think, is impacting externally by the very means of vibration. We spoke about this in the previous section of the book; it's very much a fact mostly overlooked in the mainstream.

Have you ever noticed how resonance comes into play with sound and items that it impacts upon? We have all witnessed glass being shattered at certain levels, clocks resonating to the same tick – even if they're set differently – and a whole host of other examples of sound resonance and the resulting facts from this rarely spoken about area. What may our thoughts do in this world of vibration? Even more so, what are our negative thought patterns and dismissive attitude towards research doing with the data we collect? Are we having a negative? Try not to be too robotic in your sessions, let it flow naturally.

Speak as if speaking with your friends - when you ask questions for EVP or Echovox purposes - and be kind and courteous at all times. I find this way, absolutely without a shadow of a doubt, improves results. Before your next session, think up some questions and how you may approach the task. Some pre-work in this area may just prove fruitful for you!

Watch the Gap

Try leaving a long enough gap for replies, especially as we have noticed a few seconds delay in direct hits. These gaps are crucial for communication, do not talk over the feedback or you will miss a lot! I've seen some people become so scared of the silence, they feel they must speak to get results, and this is not true. You may, by mistake, talk right over the top of some amazing proof for yourself or your organisation. It will frustrate you during analysis for sure.

Finish off Strong.

There have been instances also where people are not analysing the audio; if they do not hear it at the time, they discount the whole session. This is throwing out the baby, bath water and bath! You must upload the audio to the PC, get it into a program you can listen back with and thoroughly analyse the track. I will expand on this later for you.

Camcorder, Camera or Smartphones.

Think visual documentation rather than capturing paranormal spirits on memory card here. If you think this way, it will open up your creative side, firmly place you in the right hemisphere of the brain and assist in opening you up intuitively to the location. Leave the logic and rationality to the analysis process to follow, and just get into the feel of the place. I wish to point out at this time, that there is no need to go and buy anything special for this part. Use what you have just now; it will be more than adequate.

Most people have smartphones with good camera specifications at their fingertips - use this if it helps. Please, just turn on the aeroplane mode, so you are not disturbed, and so the EMF meters do not fluctuate due to the electromagnetic pollution being transmitted.   I currently use a DSLR Nikon 5200 for photography, a DJI OSMO for video and a DJI Drone for Aerial shots. This would be overkill for an average person getting into this type of hobby. By all means, if you plan on doing video presentations or wish to document your work on a website then do what you can with what you've got funds for. I've used everything from Smartphones to little inexpensive digital cameras. They all work perfectly for the needs at the time.

When I got to a location, I take photographs of the areas that look most attractive. I will photograph paranormal hot-spots extensively for my records, and then I will film the site in a walk around fashion. It's after this that I will begin to look into the paranormal, I always love to get that visual documentation canned and saved away before I get my hands dirty, so to speak. To recap, I'm not looking to film paranormal anomalies or catch anything, my mind is on the creative side of the brain, and I am documenting the location. If something hopefully pops up during my analysis then excellent!

Temperature Readings & Trigger Objects

I use experimental trigger objects in some locations to encourage movement, while at times I may use a laser thermometer to check the temperature of the objects for a rise or fall. When trigger objects are set, we have the ability to read the surface temperature of said objects. These objects are registered on the base test, which includes full data on the surface heat. During the observations, we can read the temperature of the object and note any abnormal fluctuations. We can also call out for any activity to be centred on the said objects and monitor any changes.

So what type of objects, you ask? This is where prior research is essential; you want to find out the history of the location and possibly of the apparition said to frequent the site. So say the deceased person loved whisky, you would hope to find little miniature bottles you could draw around. Then if they move, perhaps the apparition is trying to use energy to interact with our environment.

I've set up child chalkboards with the words "Please Write Here." I've also used toys for child sightings and old coins for historical apparitions, trying to match time frame. The prior research will unlock ideas if you wish to go down this route. Always remember, you will need an area that will not be disturbed and possibly a camcorder filming your experiment.

0.1Hz to 30Hz Brainwaves'!

7.83Hz *'Schumann resonance.'*
16.7Hz *Electric Traction Systems (Europe)*
50Hz *The building mains supply (The UK and Europe)*
60Hz *The building mains supply (USA)*
1kHz to 1MHz *Switched mode power supplies, inverters*
20kHz to 50kHz *Compact fluorescent lights (CFLs)*
150kHz to 1600kHz *AM radio broadcasts*
27MHz *CB radio*
35MHz and 40Mhz. *RC models*
88MHz to 108MHz *FM radio broadcasts*
380MHz to 400MHz *TETRA digital radio*
466MHz PMR446 *Personal 2-way radio*
470MHz to 854MHz *Television broadcasts*
800, 900, 1800 & 2100MHz 1.9GHz (1900MHz) *Cordless DECT phones*
2.4GHZ to 2.5GHz *wifi (wireless-b, -g and -n), Bluetooth, RC models, mice, doorbells...*
2.45GHz *Microwave ovens*
5.15GHz to 5.85GHz *wifi (wireless-a and -n), wireless data links and CCTV cameras*

If going to a public place, I would rarely use a trigger object as I prefer to be more light on my feet, flexible in approach and understanding of who is where and how set-ups like above may be disturbed with logical means.

EMF Meters, Energies & Hauntings

Electromagnetic energy, or EMF, is a form of energy that is reflected or emitted from objects in the form of electrical and magnetic waves that can travel through space. There are many forms of electromagnetic energy including gamma rays, x rays, ultraviolet radiation, visible light, infrared radiation, microwaves and radio waves. We see such a small percentage of the light spectrum with our eyes that detecting some forms of EMF is impossible without additional tools. This information highlights that the old saying "I will believe it when I see it." is useless in detecting reality, so must be removed from the mind set of the researcher, observer or investigator.

However, we do have tools that can measure the fluctuating waves of EM Energy, and thus, this allows us to note any occurrences in our environment accurately. Frequencies vary depending on the source of energy, and as an example, I will include a handy table to show you at what range we measure these sources.

So with all this, perhaps we should look at a tried and tested tool for measuring strange frequencies that are usually evident within locations we research.

K2 EMF Meter

This meter has become a favourite tool for all levels of researcher whether beginner or advanced. It's incredibly simple to use, with a turn on/off function and coloured LED display. The meter will sit at a steady green light setting and will progress up to the highest level, which will illuminate as red. Five LED settings show the strength of the fluctuations in the local environment. As an investigator, you will have taken what we term as base readings - see methodologies - before you begin your main session or walk around the location of interest. This way you will know your environment and will have explored the area for any normal fluctuations and thus will be prepared if anything out of the normal presents itself to you.

I use this meter on all investigations and love to have a few set up. This set-up has proven fruitful in locating any strange occurrences. In addition, I have been able to pinpoint hot spots of energy, which in turn have allowed me to gather further readings in the form of temperature fluctuations and captured audio on devices. Another cool aspect of this meter, as witnessed by many able researchers worldwide, is the blinking of the lights in response to questions we call out.

I should add at this point that these are not 'ghost detectors'. However, we could hypothesise that spirit may use AC EM Energy to attempt communication with us. To go further still, I've witnessed a collection of environmental phenomena on several devices that prove circumstantially that this is true. So in summarization, I would suggest that this tool is part of your paranormal kit, even if only to monitor the environmental changes as you go about your work. They are inexpensive and readily available on the Internet in many major countries.

Mel-Meter

Now we go a little more advanced - with an increase in needed budget - as we explore the Mel-meter and its ability to do multiple readings. Created by Gary Galka, an electrical engineer, the Mel-Meter was born because of a sad story. Gary lost his daughter Melissa in a car crash yet still felt her presence from the afterlife. This situation allowed Gary to jump into action and create several devices using his scientific qualifications to tap into the surrounding energies.

It soon became clear that it was a very useful tools and is an excellent addition to equipment used in a more advanced search of paranormal activity in the form of environmental changes and communication. If you wish a tool that can do a few neat things at once, this may be for you. Always remember to read the instructions and get to know how your tools work. Simple mistakes might invalidate your experiences and have that nasty pseudo-sceptic breathing down your neck in excitement.

Mind Set

The only thing that keeps us locked-out from further experience of the paranormal is our own perception of reality. I can go even deeper and say that the attitudes of society, mainstream science, and magicians playing the pseudo-sceptical card, tend to blinker our unique ability to experience the paranormal first-hand.

Your answers will not lay inside a peer-reviewed journal, a mainstream newspaper, or a book written by a professor hell-bent in colouring your perception to meet their views. The answers you seek will come from your ability to open your mind so wide, that you will be open to everything, but attached to nothing. Contrary to popular belief, there are no real in-depth studies done into the afterlife out with the paranormal community – no one will fund such a project, as the returns in value for their materialistic pocket is zilch. Truly, there is nothing in it for them, especially in a society where cash is king, and material possessions are a must have.

You need to view the world with new eyes, start documenting what you experience first-hand, and do not let so-called experts – who get their knowledge from textbooks or second-hand – try to define and explain away what you uncover. Start this process at local paranormal hot spots, with an open, flexible mind, and a real burning desire to find the truth. By now, you've read how consciousness works and how vibrations impact upon your reality. Make them positive vibrations, open minded, honest in application and flexible in movement when new data arises.

Whatever you do, do not allow yourself to be dragged down by pointless debates. It's a sure fire way to knocking you off course from your seeking and experiencing the non-physical.
Sceptics will scoff, and let them do so, as in my experience of working on a multitude of locations with the most experienced investigators internationally, I find no better tool than our own inner wisdom, and many of the people as mentioned earlier agree with this.

Everyone has inner wisdom, intuition, gut feelings, inner guidance, or whatever you prefer to label it. This is the internal navigation system that is your best friend on location, that will help you decide how to proceed, what to attempt, and keep your awareness on the task at hand. Subtle signs will also become evident in the form of goose bumps, slight shifts in air flow and temperature, along with peripheral vision movement, and possible full manifestation of shadows or apparitions.

You can use tools to back up what your body senses – along with the intuitive hunch – but please bear in mind that most cases of full experience – with regards to direct sighting – happen to average people with no fancy tools. Having these things will not make the chances any greater for you, they will only validate your main instrument….you yourself.

I would like you to begin tapping into the inner wisdom on location, start using it in conjunction with any tools you prefer to operate, but in accordance with the open, flexible mind set discussed, and I promise you will begin moving closer to that truth you seek. Pseudo-sceptics like to use phrases such as "If you open your mind too much, your brain will fall out" or " Extraordinary claims require extraordinary evidence." I say it is all absolute claptrap; all they are interested in is winning arguments, blinkering the possibilities through their fears of being wrong, and frankly, they have no interest in the subject unless it can make them look more intelligent than they actually are. Ignore them; this is about you and what you can find out – a positive focused mind set will stand you in good stead.

Methodologies and Getting Started

One of the hardest things to do is to put together information plans in a field so diverse that it will go against the thoughts of many who are participants within it. There is a multitude of ways to operate in this research, and at this time, no one can lay claim to a correct way of operation. Please use this section as a rough outline - not as gospel - and do not feel inclined to follow it precisely to the letter. Some of the information that you are about to read has come from investigators who have worked with my organisation International Paranormal Investigators (IPI) at various points in the last 12 years.

Highlighting Things to Keep in Mind

• Proper mind set, positive relationships and sharing.
• Continuous learning, evolving with the field and brainstorming.
• Full respect to both clients and locations.
• Common sense, exhausting natural possibilities and truthful reporting.

I wholeheartedly agree with PJay who is an IPI staff member when she said:

"I think one of the best things new people can do is ask questions. Not only ask how something is done, ask why also."

So let's say at this point that if you have any questions that you need to be answered or that you're unsure of, please do get in touch with me. There is no doubt that I will not cover every single area on such a vast topic, but I'm always available to help where I can.

Relationships

What some newcomers fail to understand is that this field is based on cooperation, not competition. We are all here for a common goal, and thus we need to have very healthy relationships with our colleagues. If you enter this field to be competitive you will not survive very long within it, we have witnessed the demise of many teams and individuals due to this.

The key to having a very successful time within the paranormal community it is to be very respectful towards all those around you. Treat everyone as your equal, learn from all the seasoned investigators who have operated at a higher level for many years and be open, honest and sharing while you operate. Remove all inclinations toward competition, negativity and related behaviours from your mind set at this point.

Those who come together in the common goal of progression within this research field tend to have very successful teams, friendships and projects. Due to the openness of their relationships and the sharing aspects that they employ in all their dealings, they become very influential in the sense that many of us take their advice and information very seriously. This behaviour is a good target to aim for if you're serious about participating in this field. More so, however, it is good to build lasting friendships while we all search for the same thing ultimately.

Learning and Application

We believe that Ian Murphy from Paranormal Research Association of Boston was spot-on when he said in one of his articles on starting a paranormal research team:

"Teams pop up all the time however a high percentage of them fail within their first year. This is generally due to bad planning, inability to manage the team and resources and inability to gain clients or their trust."

We have witnessed a plethora of teams, researchers, spiritual individuals and hobbyists fold or give up over time due to lack of planning, learning and application. To highlight: no one knows it all within this field regardless of what they say or do and how many media performances they have taken part in.

If you close your mind and are egotistical enough to believe that you know everything about investigating the paranormal, you most certainly will not be successful in your research. We are all students within this field, on different levels of experience through the knowledge we are gaining by the proper application of what we are learning. So your first steps are to locate and study a successful well-established paranormal organisation and begin your note taking and planning which in turn should be followed up by the proper action i.e. application.

Respect

We have already looked at respect in the case of colleagues and the field at large, but a crucial area is a respect to both client and locations we research. How many times have we seen newspaper articles where a group of people under the heading of "ghost hunters" have been found guilty of trespassing, damaging or breaking into a property? Worse still, we have seen a rise in clients who have been mistreated by people claiming to be researchers and proclaiming to the clients that they have X amount of spirits, vortexes or other unverified circumstances.

This has led to people fleeing their homes or being so scared that they cannot even sleep at night - this is totally unacceptable. Always be respectful to all clients, locations and under no circumstances use your title to place fear or hurt on anyone. If you're unsure, keep quiet and consult one of your peers with more knowledge within the field. If you are going solo to location, please just remember to be respectful of times you can access locations - even ruins - so as not to disturb people living close by. Never leave rubbish behind and more still, if you see litter pick it up and bin it to keep sites clean for visitors.

Common Sense

Jim Brown, IPI coordinator and an independent paranormal investigator based in the US said it beautifully when he shared the following:

"Keep your eyes, ears, and mind open."

I would also say that you should keep your common sense revved up and at the forefront of your mind while investigating, networking and operating on any level within the field. Please make it one of your top objectives to exhaust all possibilities of natural phenomena while investigating the paranormal. Do not under any circumstances ham up your field visits so as to look good or unique, this will kill your reputation stone dead when found out. It also harms the field, clients and makes a mockery of what we are trying to do as a whole. Stay true to yourself, your team and your paranormal colleagues.

What Qualifications Are Required?

None, anyone can become a paranormal investigator as there are no formal qualifications required. Don't get me wrong; you can if you wish to, jump online and find the plethora of establishments that provide their own in-house qualification. A caveat, however, that although these will give you some knowledge, there is no need for the actual certificate. Gaining a certificate or qualification is a great personal achievement but does not elevate you above anyone else in this field.

What Qualities Would Help?

Patience. Unsurprisingly this is where many newcomers fail to succeed in the field. Personally, I have sat in location for countless hours with nothing spectacular taking place but still managed to come away highly satisfied with my research. Could you do this? Be honest; it will save you a lot of time and money. In the past, I have always made the comparison of investigation with fishing due to the level of patience, setting up of equipment and then waiting for something that may never happen. I would urge a deep think about this aspect!

Also prepare yourself for countless hours of study online along with research and networking with others while your cases are active. Like it or not you will need to research, and you will need the help of others at times so good communication is a must. Your investigation does not end when you leave the location and likewise, does not begin on arrival

Get the background work done on the history, witnesses, location and pre-investigation checks. In turn, get the post work done, keep in contact with the clients and send all relevant paperwork that you promise them. Be prepared for many follow ups too.

My Location Protocol

On arrival at the location, I begin with visual documentation via DSLR Camera, Camcorder & 360 Degree Camera. I ensure I take footage and stills of all haunted hot spots and attempt to get all angles of the site. Then I send up my drone for aerial footage. Once the visual documentation of the location is complete, I decide on my specific areas of interest. This would naturally be the areas of reported sightings or any area I felt a pull towards.

My area of interest is then given a sweep with the EMF meter, taking note of any readings as a baseline. I would then place this meter in the area I felt drawn too so I could watch it while attempting a communication session. I might then decide to either use a voice recorder for pure EVP, which I may leave, set up in a discreet corner or I would set up a full ITC session. My sessions are usually limited to five-minute bursts. The reason for this is analysis, which is very lengthy.

Sometimes I do mega sessions, however, especially when with other researchers and location owners. People find it fascinating, and I feel it is only kind to oblige with longer sessions so they may gain their own evidence. I may then sit quietly for a few minutes to soak up the atmosphere and listen intently for any strange phenomena, which is usually very subtle. I pay attention to how I feel, my thinking process is observed and I certainly look out for any shivers, goosebumps or subtle movements of air. If I feel the atmosphere is engaging in the particular area I am in,I will spend more time to gain possible audio captures or direct experience, which is a key aspect for me.

I will attempt call outs, asking for any energies to communicate, move items or let themselves be known in some way. Then I repeat this till I feel the area is no longer holding an interest beyond the collection of material gained. As every location is different, some of the above may not be suitable, so I will alter it with great flexibility. If we are locked into a building overnight, I will try more experiments such as trigger objects, The methodologies do not need to be rigid, give a little flexibility and really run with how you feel at the moment.

8. Analysis & Post Investigation

So we've been to the location and conducted an overnight investigation. We've collected all our visual documentation via video and stills, noted down all our strange fluctuations and extensively worked with audio to attempt afterlife communication, now what? Well for some they leave it at this, and I must say do themselves a massive disservice by doing so. I've seen some people just upload raw audio and ask the public to let them know what's in there, what? No way?

The only way you can get away with such is if conducting a live streaming session with the public. These are sessions usually on Facebook or YouTube where you involve the public in your experiments. That's fine and total understandable and worthwhile, however, please do not do the same with your research after investigating the location whether with a team or on your own.

Audio Analysis

Listen, it's not easy, I know as I have spent countless hours analysing audio files and it can be a tedious job to complete. Every five minutes of captured ITC audio takes a good hour to power through, as you need to alter the file speed and sometimes clarity via different filters. Oh, but how it's worth it when you get something out of the ordinary. Listening back and hearing clear names, history details and, sometimes, colourful language can be an entertaining process, to say the least.

So upload that file to your PC or laptop and prepare to work for an hour or so on your captured audio files. I use Adobe Audition for this as it has the features I'm looking for, which include the ability to see graphics, slow things down, reverse audio that sounds backwards and isolates sound that stands out. You may want to use a free program such as Audacity which can still do the job. Just getting it into the program and fully checking it is the key; what you use to do so, is up to you.

My tips for finding the captures would be to have patience and to slow down the audio. When you use a program such as Echovox, you will notice that some of the captures are just so fast - even with the setting slow at the session - and you will miss a lot without slowing it down. Do not get me wrong; some captures are as clear as day. However, there will be some golden nuggets deep within the chatter. I remember pulling out one capture on analysis after returning from a Pittenweem investigation. I had asked "Do You See Me." and just a few seconds later you hear a clear but quiet "I see you." I must say I was utterly flabbergasted at the clarity of the capture, but more so, I was so relieved that I had done a full analysis of the files. What a missed catch that would have been!

So get the audio into your program, slow it down and listen carefully. Especially when using Echovox or Voxbox files! Using standard audio files in search for EVPs is challenging but not as difficult as wading through Echovox files. The problem is losing focus, patience and that all too familiar feeling of wishing to skip through the file. We've all been there. You must stick it out though as again you may miss something that just blows your mind and adds to your collection of interesting audio captures.

My tip here would be volume boost; some EVPs are so quiet, and you must be laser focussed on hearing them, with the additional tip of listening for any strange clicks. Why the latter? Well, let's just say that a unique pattern has been noticed when finding amazing EVP's on the files and it always seems to be either before or after a unique clicking sound. I'm completely unsure of why this is, of course, I have my thoughts, but nevertheless, it seems to be a noise that accompanies some interesting phenomena. Listen out for it and let me know if you find the same as me with this.

So to recap on this topic of audio analysis.

- We are going to upload all out files to our desktop and load it into our software of choice. We are going to slow down Echovox type files and carefully listen to each exciting sound.

If we use standard files from an audio capture device, we will do likewise. However, we will boost the sound, stay focused and listen for any strange clicking noises especially.

Feel free to share all your captures with us online, you can find me on my Haunted Scotland Facebook page or in the Scottish Paranormal group. I will happily listen and give some feedback where I can.

Checking Historical Information Against Captures

Try not to do this before you begin the analysis process; I am aware you will have already done some pre-investigation work, but do not revisit it till you analyse. Let me explain: When you begin to pull out words and phrases from your audio files, it's good practice to open a mini-research session into each and every capture. In doing so, you may link firm evidence of names, places and dates to the site you've just investigated.

This provides solid evidence of spirit communication for you as a person, and for others, you may wish to share your findings with. However, if you begin to pull down the location data just before you start the analysis of audio, there is a slight chance you will interpret some words to fit into the research, this is not good practice and will invalidate your results. It's similar to keeping information away from Mediums you may take on location, to keep their mind clear and rule out any accusations from outside - you put controls in place.

Do the same with your audio analysis, clear the mind and go without any preconceived ideas or thought. I do wish to impress upon you the habit of checking all your audio captures when done, however. See if you may have connected names, dates, local locations or information that links your work to the place of interest. Include this information in your articles, videos or information you share with others. It's an excellent habit to get into and will elevate your work greatly.

Checking Photographs and Video Files

As mentioned previously, I do not take visual recordings with the intent of capturing paranormal activity at a location I visit. These are used solely as a visual documentation of the site for video presentations, website articles and my files for future revisits and resulting reports. That's not to say that you can't capture something paranormal.

There are a few things I need to highlight, as it's an area of confusion for some members of the public who contact my colleagues or myself. That is the topic of Orbs aka light anomalies. As we increase our technology with the invention of digital photography, we've seen an increase in light anomalies captured under a whole host of circumstances. Little balls of light that some mistake as absolute proof of paranormal activity.

Extensive testing has been completed by many very able researchers in this area of orbs and light anomalies, and it's something where we can reproduce a good 95% plus by mimicking certain conditions. As an example: Taking pictures with the flash on can reflect light back into the lens producing small semi-translucent orbs. This is due to natural phenomena such as insects, dust, pollen or even water vapour. This is not to say that all light anomalies are the above, it's to make you aware that a very high percentage will fall under that bracket.

I rarely use the flash on my equipment - I prefer natural lighted imagery - so I rarely get natural particles polluting my pictures. I mean, of course, the sunlight can cause the same effect at times, but you do become wise to it. Sunlight - and lights indoors - can also cause lens flare, which will cause large circular anomalies which are usually a purple hue. These are easily identified at the time, as they will move with your movement of the device you use. These are sometimes passed off as paranormal in nature, when they are natural occurrences that will haunt your stunning shots when not setting up your photograph correctly.

Then the next natural capture to be careful of is motion blur. Motion blur is where you move your camera while taking a longer exposure, usually where light levels are low, and the camera needs to use a more prolonged exposure for the light. If something moves within your long exposure masterpiece, you will also gain a motion blur of said object or person.

So a few things to be careful of when doing the analysis of your visual documentation files:

1. Flash On Camera: Where rain, snow, dust, pollen and insects may be present.

Flash On Camera: Where mist, cold air or smokers have been, which will cause a misting effect.

Lens Flare: Strong light source reflects into the camera, it will move with your movements.

Motion Blur: Fast moving wildlife, people or objects causing a ghosting effect.

Motion Blur: Where low light creates a longer exposure and you move the camera too fast, or even slightly while in extremely low light.

This is not to say that paranormal activity cannot be captured, even in the form of self-illuminating anomalies (Orbs) or shadow figures for that matter. I've seen some fascinating captures in my time that can be classed as paranormal. Yes, they still get scrutinised and declared false by some - this always happens - but to a plethora of proper researchers, we can see the uniqueness in such captures.

My suggestion would be to upload all your images and video files to desktop and check them all. Discard any natural phenomena type material, keep your best shots and then share them. If you feel you may have something that is not natural, get in contact with a few different researchers and ask their honest opinion on them. Get a variety of views. However, we are all different in our thinking so never settle for one opinion.

For photography I use Lightroom, but Windows does have their own image viewer that you can zoom in and study your files. For video I use PowerDirector for creative work, this allows me to review my files too. At times, I use Windows Media Player just to scan through the material.

Revisiting the Location

The astonishing thing I find about some investigators is their reluctance to go back to a location for further research. Seriously, I know some who prefer new locations each time, rather than building upon their hard work and analysis. I have always been of the mind that an alleged haunted location should be monitored over several visits, even altering time, conditions and period of the year to expand on possible differences of activity - if any - and to increase the data collection process. In the upcoming chapters on locations, you will see that some sites I visit yearly which so far adds up to over ten visits. If a location is closer to me and I can pop out to it for more data, I will.

The first visit to a place is your introduction to that case; you are learning all the experiences of the witnesses, the layout of the site and tracking down the hot spots of paranormal activity. You are collecting visual documentation, environmental data and audio files for the first time too, and as soon as you analyse this data, you WILL find that a return visit is needed.

Let's start with audio captures. While analysing our files, we may gain a collection of words or phrases that make little sense to us, and we wish to find out more about. The best way to do this is to revisit for more sessions. You would take your captures - perhaps names - and construct these into your new questions as you begin to dig deeper. On the return, you can ask more questions about the answers already gained. This process then begins to expand your audio captures, your evidence and you are obtaining answers to the activity that is present at the location. Likewise, you may have images or footage that show something strange, perhaps a shadow figure or someone at a window, which you were sure, was not there, so a return is going to be crucial.

A prime example of this is the image shared by Chris Aitchison from Tantallon Castle, which turned up in various newspapers. It appeared to show a figure in a ruff and period costume, peering out of the window on the upper floor. It's said Chris contacted the castle to ask if anyone had been in costume this day, where he was told no re-enactments were in play.

The image was placed in the unexplained category and became a hot topic of debate online between the believer, sceptics and paranormal investigators. Some debunkers even attempted to come up with fanciful explanations of light reflections and how believers were not rational in their approach. They went to massive length to debunk, which included insults and an attitude of looking down their nose at all those with an interest.

I took the bull by the horns and directly went to the location on a lovely sunny day, knowing I could get a nice so-called light reflection into the bargain. I photographed the window from all sorts of angles, but especially the exact angle of the original picture and thus, was able to turn the tables and completely debunk the debunkers. As I suspected, their explanation was claptrap, and the visit to the location proved this. Regardless of the sun shining and reflecting in the particular window area, including shadows and people walking via the exact area, nothing reproduced the photograph to a satisfactory level.

This highlights my point that trying to do analysis without doing the physical work on location is not a real investigation, research or any use to the cases in question. It can be highly beneficial to go back to the site where any interesting evidence was gained and do further probing, rather than leaving assumptions hanging over the case. Return visits at regular periods can be massively beneficial to your research or personal experiences. Single visits may give a basic overview, but if you wish some depth then for the reasons mentioned above, I would get all the data together, construct a fresh plan and then get back on site.

8. Haunted Castles

Aberdour Castle

The Kingdom of Fife is the setting for this stunning historical castle; to be more precise, Aberdour is located at coastal village of Easter Aberdour that sits across the River Forth from the Scottish capital city of Edinburgh. It's mindblowing to think that parts of Aberdour Castle date from approximately 1200, making it one of the two oldest datable castles from within Scotland, the other being Castle Sween, in Argyll. The earliest parts of Aberdour Castle once comprised of a very modest hall house, which once sat overlooking the Dour Burn. Expansion took placeover the following 400 years that massive expansion. The hall house became a tower house around the 15th century, undergoing a further two expansions during the 16th century, according to historical information

The Castle is mostly the creation of the Douglas Earls of Morton, who held Aberdour from the 14th century. The Douglas Earls - a very powerful Scottish family - used Aberdour Castle as a second home until around 1642, when their primary residence, Dalkeith House, was sold. In 1725 the family purchased nearby Aberdour House, and the medieval castle was unfortunately allowed to fall into decay. Today, only the 17th-century wing remains roofed, while the tower has mostly collapsed. It is within this roofed part of the castle; a stunning well cared for monument of historical significance, that things a little more non-physical seem to transpire.

Paranormal Activity

Quite a few years ago, in the depths of winter, a group of stonemasons and labourers stood in the stables of Aberdour Castle. As they stood – chatting about the usual topics – they hunched their bodies up against the biting cold wind that whistled through the stable door. Suddenly the conversation all stopped.

"Do you hear that?" enquired one of the labourers.

The workers all now stood deathly still, straining to hear whatever it was their friend had heard coming from the Great Hall up above. They didn't have to wait long, as a loud dragging noise was heard by all present.

"Somebody's moving the furniture about up there in the Hall." The young apprentice said.

They all looked at each other now quite alarmed, had someone somehow managed to get into the castle during the night? And if they had, were they still in there?

The workers stood now pondering what their next move should be, should they ring the police, or wait for the custodian to arrive? The time was now 9.12 am, so after a quick discussion, they decided to wait for the custodian to come, electing to post a guard at all three exits from the Hall, while others stood by the stable door awaiting the arrival of the custodian. A few minutes later the sound of a car was heard coming up the driveway; it was Dawn, the custodian.

They very quickly related their version of events to her, she being extremely dubious of the story, which she was now hearing. She asked them to take a key each and unlock all the doors to the Hall at the same time. Once again, the noise from the hall was heard, this time Dawn heard it also. Their faces pale with either fright or anticipation of fear, they all now headed toward the exits. As they reached them, they all yelled out loud and simultaneously opened the doors to the Great Hall. What they saw chilled them to the bone.

The Great Hall of Aberdour Castle contains replica medieval furniture that was, by its very design, extremely heavy and cumbersome, even a small table required two persons to move it. It was, therefore, a shock to see this all furniture now moved in its entirety into the middle of the room. And as for the doors, the only means of entry and exit to the Hall, they were all locked as were all the windows. No one knows who or what moved the furniture, many think it might be the spirit of the Fourth Earl of Morton, but there are many contenders for the ghost of Aberdour Castle.

My Visits

I've briefly worked at this location - for Historic Scotland - and have researched the history and stories extensively. Outwith this, I've also wandered the site on many occasions, recording the environment sounds. Even while I worked here, I've always had the feeling that I was carefully watched by something not seen or felt by the physical senses. I'm unsure if this is because I know of the tales as mentioned above, or whether some interactive sentient apparition does in fact still wander the Great Hall and surrounding rooms.

I've captured various ghostly sounds when no other visitors have been present, as I walked the areas in silence, trying to feel the environment and tune into the feel of the location. Of note, through these audio captures, the names "Prisbrey" and "Bruce" have come up and been stored in the Haunted Scotland files for Aberdour.

When I asked if anyone was there, I also received the reply, "Could be."

A little more alarming is the capture, "Get him!" This I will surmise was aimed at my wandering of the area with my audio capture devices.

The energies are undoubtedly present, but why, we will never know. It also appears that they are sentient energies at that, for the audio captures seem to display intelligence that can see the physical from the non-physical world.

Aberdour Castle
Aberdour,
Fife
KY3 0SL

Blackness Castle

Historian and former *Most Haunted* regular, Richard Jones, described Blackness Castle as the worst paranormal site he had visited.

"It terrified me!" he stated.

This one always held me intrigued, and I've visited a fair few times. Situated on the Firth of Forth, Blackness Castle was built in the 15th century by the Crichtons - an incredibly powerful

Scottish family – but was eventually annexed by James II, later becoming a royal residence. Blackness is often called 'the ship that never sailed' as it looks like a great ship that has run aground. It's sharp stem points toward the water, while the square stern stands beached on dry land, your access point into the property. Three towers add to the effect, a small tower at the prow, a tall central tower that projects like the main mast of a ship and a solid tower at the rear.

The Castle played its part in history as a prison, housing some high-ranking individuals, it became a formidable stronghold with thickened walls and defensive guns.. Many high-status prisoners were held here in later medieval times. The most famous was Cardinal David Beaton, Archbishop of St Andrews, in 1543. Beaton was for a long time one of the main rivals of the Earl of Arran, who was Regent of Scotland when Mary Queen of Scots was an infant. The Castle was also held in support of Mary Queen of Scots for six years

Blackness was besieged by Cromwell in 1650 who left the Castle in ruins. In the 1670's and 1680's - known as the 'Killing Times' - Charles II and James VII locked up many Covenanters at Blackness Castle. Later, around the 1700's, Blackness was used as a prison for foreign soldiers and sailors, who were captured during the wars with Spain, France and the fledgeling USA. It was restored during the Napoleonic Wars when it again served as a prison. Blackness was intended to be a suitable residence for imprisoned nobleman, whilst the reigning sovereign would use it chiefly as a garrison stronghold and a state prison. Blackness Castle was to be decommissioned after the First World War, whereas afterwards it would be passed into state care as a visitor attraction.

Paranormal Activity

While it's not overly publicised, there have been reports of unexplained noises emanating from within the Castle. We also have a report of a Knight, one who seems to be overly angry at the presence of people visiting the Central Keep. In the late 1990's, a woman and her two young sons were visiting, when she was startled by the sudden appearance of the Knight, in armour, whom she claimed chased her angrily from the tower. Allegedly, a group of paranormal enthusiasts, who persuaded the custodian to allow them to stay overnight on Halloween, were disturbed by the constant noise of furniture being scraped and banged across the stone floor of the room beneath them.

This type of phenomena is very much common, with similar reported from Aberdour Castle as previously mentioned. On investigating, the paranormal enthusiasts found that nothing was out of place. However, the noises re-commenced the moment they returned to their companions.

My Visits

I have to say I'm not surprised in the slightest at the reports from the Castle, as it's certainly a very atmospheric location. There are so many areas to explore and investigate at Blackness; there were points where I found myself in dark areas with that all too familiar shiver down the spine. Nevertheless, a job was to be done – and material to be gathered – so onwards I travelled within the warren of rooms with offshoot nooks and crannies.

The question is, did I witness anything? Well, in all honesty, nothing that I could not attribute to the blustery winds that blew along the estuary and bombarded the tower and walls.

I spent some time in the stairwell of the mast tower prison, in this area it was evident that strange banging, creaking and groaning could be heard. I further investigated in January 2014,with the windows being the prime suspect for the various bangs and thuds. Audio recordings - as always - would become significant here, with various voices captured on devices. What was imprinting the names and requests we found?

All in all, I have to say I thoroughly enjoyed both visits to Blackness Castle. I found the curator to be an excellent help, taking his time to brief us on the history of this magnificent stronghold fully.Incredible scenery, a warren of areas to explore, and a sense of standing within historic walls, I would urge anyone in the area to visit the marvellous Historic Scotland property.

Its paranormal secrets will need to stay as such, at least until my next visit, where I may just probe that little bit further. Time will tell

Blackness Castle
Blackness,
Linlithgow
EH49 7NH

Glamis Castle

Situated beside the village of Glamis, this was the childhood home to the Queen Mother, and is still home to the Earl and Countess of Strathmore and Kinghorne. The estate surrounding the Castle covers more than 57 square kilometres (14,000 acres) and, in addition to parks and gardens, it also produces several cash crops including lumber and beef. The vicinity of Glamis Castle has pre historic traces; for example, a noted intricately carved Pictish stone – known as the Eassie Stone – was found in a creek-bed at the nearby village of Eassie.

Like much of Angus, the area is rich in history, and the lands indeed date back to the Pictish people. Glamis Castle is known as one of the most haunted castles in Britain and is it any wonder with the abundance of well known historical figures who have attended this location? Where we find such history and emotional connections, we find a plethora of strange activity.

Paranormal Activity

The family chapel is alleged to be haunted by what people describe as a Grey Lady, who is said to be the spirit of Lady Janet Douglas, who was burned at the stake as a witch on Castle Hill, in Edinburgh around 1537. King James V of Scotland did not favour the powerful Douglas family due to him being imprisoned by Archibald Douglas, 6th Earl of Angus who was Janets Brother. The King was only 14 years old, and all attempts to free him were foiled, until March 1528, when the young King James escaped custody and took refuge at Stirling.

He clearly was not to forget his foes, the Douglases, as nine years later he would accuse Janet of witchcraft, even though it was evident the accusation was indeed false. To gain the evidence that he would require, James had Janet's family members and her servants subjected to torture. Janet was convicted and then burned at the stake on 17 July 1537 on the Esplanade at Edinburgh Castle. A number of witnesses have seen her apparition at the chapel and the

Clock Tower at Glamis Castle. Janet is not the only apparition spotted at this location.

The spirit of a woman with a missing tongue is said to haunt the grounds. She allegedly runs around the estate pointing at her supposedly mutilated face. Perhaps she is trying to tell us a tale so her spirit can move on in peace? Inside the castle, we have more spooky activity.

A young black boy, the ghost of a servant from around 200 years ago, haunts a stone seat by the door of the Queen's bedroom. Why he is here, no one knows.

One of the more infamous spirits is known as Earl Beardie, allegedly a cruel and wicked man, probably stemming from his rebellion against King James II. His apparition is said to wander the castle, and there have been reports of children waking to find his figure leaning over their beds.

My Visit

I feel honoured that I've had the opportunity to investigate, research and report on the paranormal activity of Glamis Castle. The castle is not open to paranormal research groups, and this is most likely due to the need to keep the castle integrity intact away from the flood of requests due to popular programs such as *Most Haunted*. There was a time when Paranormal TV programs were at their height, that everyone with interest was setting up investigations without knowing how to conduct them. So many locations closed their doors to these teams, to allow their properties to keep their integrity, protect the history and prestige of such structures and continue in their areas of expertise, which was not the topic of the paranormal.

Glamis Castle being classed as a prestigious location with such deep history and still, a family residence was not different. It had a reputation as the most haunted castle in the world, and with that, they were inundated with requests from TV and worldwide groups. It would take me ten years to gain access, perhaps I had to prove my passion and professionalism, but none the less when I had the opportunity to conduct some research on the grounds finally and around the building, I was delighted. I ran through my usual protocols for public place research, which had to be mindful of the public enjoying their visit here, and I ensured I gathered as much data as possible. So as soon as the visual documentation was complete, helped by a stunning warm day, I moved on to the gardens and conducted some audio recordings.

I managed to catch a few voices, which can be found online on the website and YouTube channel, but the stand out ones were:

"I've Been Put Here"

"Talking Out Mouth."

"You Tell Me?"

"I'm Scared."

So it was a rather fruitful visit on the first attendance at Glamis Castle. At the time, I never knew I would be back with a French production company, only I would be inside this time.

My email goes consistently with many requests to do certain projects. Some will grab my attention, while others I will pass over to colleagues. When I saw the opportunity to return to Glamis Castle with France2, a large French broadcaster, I grabbed the chance and went ahead with the project. This was finally my chance to enter the stunning castle in a paranormal project, something I had visualised for over ten years.

I would need backup on this one, due to the amount of equipment I planned to take and for some thorough help in the mini investigation. So I called on Lynne Knight and Stephen King, both close colleagues I conduct research with and people I could trust 100% in this delicate project. I want to highlight a couple of areas with this one; something picked up by all of us while we entered the Castle. The first instance was the Curator attempting to turn the lights on so we could climb the steep stairs to the attic, however, when he went to do so, the lights blew leaving us in semi-darkness. Interesting I thought!

It was a common occurrence according to our guide; the light go rather often. Even more interesting I thought. The next one was the rather unusual EMF readings wede pick up while conducting more audio experiments, long with some faint banging too. During the audio analysis, which is also online, we again had a few interesting captures from inside Glamis Castle.

After asking for energies, we received the following responses:

"Hallway"

"In Bunker"

And a rather lovely "Come Here."

The name "Glamis" did also come over the audio.

I did feel as if we were being watched inside Glamis Castle; I also feel the location holds many secrets and much more activity may transpire to visitor and staff alike. It certainly holds up to its reputation in my eyes, Glamis Castle is a jewel in the crown of Scotland, in that, there is no doubt. Hopefully I will be invited back to continue my research into the unseen worlds at such prestigious locations.

Glamis Castle
Angus
DD8 1RJ

Hailes Castle

Nestled within the countryside of East Lothian, away from the more well-known Edinburgh haunted hot-spots,many people miss Hailes Castle completely on their visit to Scotland or underestimate its beauty along with that all too familiar mix of paranormal activity. This may not be underground Edinburgh or the grandeur of Glamis Castle, but make no mistake, the witness testimonies of ghostly behaviour are every bit as significant and of keen interest. Hailes Castle is a 14th century castle about a mile and a half south-west of East Linton, in East Lothian. The castle has an excellent riverside setting.

Hailes Castle was first built by the de Gourlay family approximately in the early 1200s. The de Gourlays lost the Castle in the 1300s, allegedly due to their close association with the Balliol family. The Balliols were at war with King Edward of England, and ultimately lost the battle for the crown of Scotland during these Wars of Independence between the two countries. The Hepburn family became the Lords of Hailes, in the aftermath. The Castle was allegedly damaged severely during the wars, and along with Dirleton and Yester (Goblin Ha), Hailes was said to have been another of the three East Lothian castles to have been sacked.

James Hepburn, who was the 4th earl of Bothwell was born at Hailes Castle in 1535. He became the third husband of Mary Queen of Scots. Mary stayed at Hailes Castle on the way from

Dunbar to the wedding held at Holyroodhouse in Edinburgh on May 5, 1567.

Paranormal Activity

Deep from within the walls of the Castle, various banging and moving sounds have been reported, though no clear visual data accompanies these sounds as yet. Many il further innvestigated in January 2014,with the windows being the prime suspect for the various bangs and thuds.nvestigation & research teams, along with members of the public, have commented on this phenomena. Due to the connection between Mary Queen Of Scots and Hailes Castle, there is some speculation that the next apparition may be her. The activity at this location includes the sighting of a Lady in White, rumoured to be the much travelled Mary Queen of Scots, however, not every White Lady needs to be connected to this much seen historical figure.

Past family members from the castle, staff who once worked here, or local people long gone could be connected to this apparition. The figure is said to float through the Castle and its grounds graciously. The apparition has often sighted by both visitors to the area and locals alike throughout the years, right up to the present. During one visit to the Castle while accompanied by a visitor to Scotland, we heard the sound of small stones falling at the entry way to the vaulted area. We could say the stones were being thrown, but we do not know that for certain.

Incidentally, it did coincide with us telling stories about the area, the atmosphere was electric at the time, and it was very much happening in real-time.

My Visit

I make an effort to visit this castle every year as I find it absolutely stunning. I'm in awe at the peace and quiet I feel as I wander the grounds.I run through those all too familiar protocols when I arrive, with the added bonus of having a lovely picnic in the grounds. So as soon as the visual documentation is canned, It's an intense audio session followed by a bite to eat.

I've not encountered the Lady in White floating through the grounds yet, but I hold out hope of encountering her at some point in the future.What I've certainly encountered, however, is audio captures that blew my mind. I've heard the 'Hepburn' family name being called - you can hear this online - along with a whole host of fascinating captures around the area of the pit-prison. I've also experienced physical activity here with various knocks, bangs and stones being thrown in the undercroft kitchen area. Let's be clear too that this happened in the company of others, who were astonished, and not just while on my own

So, I would urge readers to take a trip here if they can, it's free to enter, and it will be a lovely day out for all. I have to end this one with congratulations to Historic Scotland who keep these grounds in pristine condition for us all.

Hailes Castle
Haddington
EH41 4PY

Norham Castle

Named "The Most Dangerous Castle in England" due to its strategic position, overlooking the River Tweed and within close proximity to Scotland, Norham is partly ruined but in surprisingly good condition and well looked after by the English Heritage. This can be seen by the well-kept lawns and lack of litter in this stunning location. As you can imagine, the Castle saw much action during the wars between England and Scotland. To list a number of times it was besieged, captured then returned, would cause a long read indeed.

The Castle came to be when Ranulf Flambard, who was the Bishop of Durham from 1099 to 1128, gave orders for its construction in 1121. This was with a view to protecting the property of the Bishopric in north Northumberland, from further incursions by what they termed the pesky Scots. In 1136, King David I of Scotland invaded neighbouring Northumberland and Norham Castle. It was quickly handed back to the Bishopric but was recaptured in 1138 during yet another invasion. The Castle stands on the south bank of the River Tweed, elevated above the river so that the north side is protected by a steep slope. A deep ravine protected the Castle's east side, and an additional artificial moat were dug round the west and south sides to complete the protection.

Paranormal Activity

The only report we have to date with regards to paranormal activity at Norham Castle, is that of a Grey Lady, who is supposedly resident within the castle grounds. Who can this apparition be? With such visitors as the wife of Longshanks, Kind Edward of England, there are many ladies of importance from which to pick. Then again, the spirits of humble maids and general staff may be wandering the grounds after the gruesome captures by the Scots in times gone by, now looking for some closure in the afterlife.

My Research

I had take a long drive south and cross the border into England for this one. However, I was not disappointed in the slightest. This visit was in conjunction with my good friend and amazing researcher, Christopher Huff, of Durham. Not only is he a very able researcher, but also an amazing published author with more than 40 years' experience of all things mystical.

During the investigation, observation and recording sessions, we utilised many tools such as audio recording devices, P-SB7, Echovox along with visual documentation and environmental energy data. I find Chris to have said it perfectly when he shared the following report - including mediumistic impressions - after we finished our initial look at this Castle.

Chris' Report

Arriving at 10 am afforded the opportunity for a good walk around and photo session before we were due to begin.

The first impression was of two women, one with long dark hair and one with red/gold/blond hair, the first in a blue dress and the latter in a red dress of perhaps 13th century style. The woman in the red dress had a gold circlet on her hair, and the braided style of hair that she wore had a sort of gold braid mesh over.

There was an apparent bustle going on, and these women, the one in the red dress, in particular, was ensuring that everything was going to be perfect for a Royal (?) visit. In particular, she was examining apples making sure that none were wrinkled or bad

There was a definite presence in the area of the half covered undercroft, where we later performed the P-SB7 session and another half way up the spiral stairs.

On the first floor, there was a man with cropped, ragged and none too clean black hair, stocky build with a black beard close cropped and dark eyes. He wore a dark coloured leather tunic with what seemed to be studs or plates on it. He didn't seem too happy that we were there.

Looking over the courtyard, the wall nearest to the Tweed (and Scotland) was seen rebuilt and with men in surcoats or livery fighting desperately along the top; ladders were pitched against the outside and men in ragged costume were swarming over the wall.

Slightly later, looking down into the undercroft mentioned above, there were heaps of bodies on men in surcoats possibly slaughtered there

On the first floor, there were also the impressions of the ragged men running amok and taking anything that wasn't nailed down - and some things that were – even things of no value were being carried off as prizes

While up on this floor I turned and saw out of the corner of my eye a female form in the alcove next to the stair. Although she vanished immediately, I managed to make spirit contact with a dishevelled, dirty teenager who was hiding and peering at us, hugging the wall in fear of us.

Eventually I received the story that she had been raped many times and then had her throat cut, interestingly after having received this information she tended to follow us around the keep and into the

EVP, etc. sessions. I hope that in some small way we have helped her to pass on a bit

At a later stage, there was a large body of surcoated men who marched into what seemed like a deserted castle and formed up in the courtyard.

So as you can see, such a positive visit to Norham Castle, a location that provided us with so much data, audio and feedback from my colleagues. Like all inclusions I share here, you can check out our videos and captures online.

Norham Castle,
Berwick-upon-Tweed
TD15 2JY

9. Religious Haunts

Balmerino Abbey

At the top of the Kingdom Of Fife, before you approach and cross the Tay Estuary, you will find a little village the holds a great secret. This secret is well nestled within the village, a former monastic centre in Fife, it's a hidden abbey of great significance in history. Balmerino Abbey was a Cistercian founded community Abbey which dates back to approximately 1227.

It's well documented that there's a strong connection between the Monks from Melrose Abbey, King Alexander II of Scotland, and this stunning location. You can almost feel the history as you wander the grounds with this place.

Founded in 1227 to 1229 by monks from Melrose Abbey, with the patronage of Ermengarde de Beaumont and King Alexander II of Scotland, Balmerino Abbey is genuinely historic.It remained a daughter house of Melrose Abbey and had approximately 20 monks, still in position, at the beginning of the 16th century, but ultimately began to decline in the same century. In December 1547 it was allegedly burned by an English force and allegedly damaged again in 1559 by Scottish Protestants. Balmerino was, therefore, no stranger to aggression by outside forces.

Balmerino Abbey became a dwelling house of the lords Balmerino after secularisation in 1603. It was converted to a barony and occupied by generations of the Lords of Balmerino.

Paranormal Activity

Witnesses report ghostly monks floating throughout the grounds of Balmerino Abbey. Allegedly they can still be seen pushing wheelbarrows around the grounds as if still working for the community. We're unsure where exactly, or whether this is at random spots around the Abbey., I would heavily suggest that this activity is of a non-sentient type - as discussed in previous chapters - so any interaction attempts would be futile.

This kind of activity, however, does not take away from the awe of witnessing such a spectacle. It truly is a wonder to see history play out before your eyes in such a place as this.

In the central Keep, there's said to be a spirit who sits and checks the corn for mice and rats. Again, rather than an active energy with sentient characteristics, this sounds more like a non-sentient replay enacted for the conscious observer who witnesses it.

Somehow, the observing consciousness - the witness - is causing a spark in the environment that allows the replay to enact the event. It may be as simple as the emotional state of the witness is ripe for such occurrences, or the brain is in some way dropping the limitations of the physical senses, and the witness consciousness is freely expanding into areas of the unseen.

My Visits

I have visited this location for over ten years now, usually trying to get there every year to update my records and to update the public through my Haunted Scotland website and Facebook page. I've never been let down while here.

Firstly, the location is well maintained by The National Trust Of Scotland. If there to visit, leave donations in the box provided - it is such a peaceful day out with stunning views over the Tay estuary. I must emphasise that no matter your thoughts on the afterlife, places such as this are an absolute joy to spend time in. I would recommend this as an area to take the family, enjoy a picnic and where you can sit back in peace and soak up the atmosphere.

I mean it when I say you can feel the history, a certain vibe of importance as you wander such places. In addition to this one, however, you can also, at times, feel as if you are being watched. Something I've picked up on several occasions in the past. It's a small location, so conducting visual documentation is done fairly quickly, which allows you to get into the bones of the research. I would suggest a session of audio in the little undercroft situated to the left of the tree at the back of the site. This area seems to prove excellent for audio captures; it's sheltered which helps massively, and you can monitor the Abbey building from afar.

It's dangerous at the Abbey, and thus it's fenced off for the safety of the public; this is not a detriment to your visit though, as you can still see all areas perfectly fine from the fence. Spirit is not confined to a zone, if active here; they can move.So what have I uncovered here?

Well, it's one of the few areas where I've never encountered out of the ordinary Electromagnetic fluctuations, which strengthens the evidence at other places. If my equipment were the lone source of such phenomenon- measuring the AC - then this would be a stable result across the plethora of locations I've looked at spanning many years. Audio is a different story, however, and we have not been let down at this site. Catches of note include:

"You Have Brought"
"Derek Took The Debt"
"Drop Dead"
& "Stupid Men."

As we can see, these are not just single words of may sound like proportions; these are actual phrases as if some type of intelligence is trying to communicate with us. I am entirely unsure of what they are trying to communicate with me, Yet, I feel a simple trip back with more probing in this area may prove some more depth to this. Perhaps you could make the trip if near enough and let us know what you can uncover? Could this mean we have an interactive consciousness in this Abbey then? Perhaps so, as we certainly have an attempted communication.

Balmerino Abbey is such a historic location that I am not surprised in the slightest; I will return and provide more evidence from here, not forgetting a lovely picnic with our unseen friends.

Balmerino Abbey,
Balmerino Village,
Newport-on-Tay
DD6 8SB

Cambuskenneth Abbey

I must say, this is my favourite part of Scotland and I have absolutely no idea why, I only know I feel very drawn to the Stirling area and the historical nature of the lands. Whether this is due to great battles at places nearby such as Bannockburn, where a great Scottish victory for Robert The Bruce gave Scotland her independence, or the amazing locations with such awe-inspiring atmospheres, it doesn't matter, the area is stunning. Cambuskenneth village with her historical abbey comes under the above on two fronts, atmosphere and history.

Cambuskenneth Abbey is a mostly ruined Augustinian monastery situated near Stirling in Scotland. The Abbey sits in the shadows of both Stirling Castle, and the Wallace Monument, then a little further still we reach the famous location of Bannockburn. All these locations have connections to the Abbey, which shows its historical significance to the area.

Founded around the year 1140 by King David I of Scotland, originally it was named the Abbey of St Mary of Stirling. One of the more famous abbeys of Scotland in its time – due in part to its proximity to the Royal Burgh of Stirling – the location was no stranger to historical situations.

Royalty – surprisingly including Edward Longshanks, King of England and less surprisingly Robert the Bruce, King of Scotland – prayed regularly at the Abbey. The Bruce even held his Parliament here in 1326 to confirm the succession of his son David II. In 1486 Margaret of Denmark died at nearby Stirling Castle and was buried at Cambuskenneth Abbey. Then in 1488, the body of her husband James III – who was murdered at the Battle of Sauchieburn – was taken to Cambuskenneth Abbey for his burial.

The Abbey then fell into disuse during the Scottish Reformation, and by 1559 the Abbey was closed, and the buildings allegedly looted and burned. Cambuskenneth was placed under the jurisdiction of the military governor at Stirling Castle, who is said to have had the stonework used in construction projects in the Castle.

Further intrigue can be found in a local story with regards to William Wallace's left arm and this location. After he was executed, his body parts were sent to various places as a warning to others His left arm would find itself in Stirling. When the flesh had fallen away, it is said that the monks from Cambuskenneth Abbey went in the dead of night and collected it. Returning to the Abbey, they buried it outstretched and pointing towards Abbey Craig, the site of what is now the Wallace Monument.

Paranormal Activity

Witnesses have reported seeing the shadowy figures of the monks at this location. Usually, they are spotted on the first floor of the tower, and at times on the turnpike stair. We are unsure if these are interactive apparitions or more a residual replay of times gone-by.
The ghost of James III and Queen Margaret have also been seen on the grounds here, not surprising since they loved this location so much and are buried here too. Could it be their energies visiting due to a strong emotional connection to the area, or again, are we looking at possible residual replays?

Mary, Queen of Scots – Yes I know, she is everywhere – was crowned at Stirling in 1542 and her ghost is said to walk the grounds here too. Our Queen has been seen in a plethora of locations across this land; I would, therefore, argue that this is residual energy mostly and that the strong emotional connection to sites is what has somehow embedded itself into our environment.

Most certainly this Abbey is a hotbed for activity, and one often overlooked in favour of the more well-known locations in this historically rich part of Scotland. How would I get on as I wandered the grounds, recording the atmosphere while feeling the area for strange sensations, and scanning for audio in the hope of coherence via the audio software?

My Visit.

I've had two visits here so far, which is rather light to give a definite conclusion regarding the reported hauntings. However, this is certainly better than the single visit I had right up until I finished this section of the book, as I have just returned from here once more. I was in awe at the craftmanship of the Abbey and was lucky enough to be there at the same time as a gentleman who knew a fair bit about its construction.

He informed me of the history in construction by Stonemasons with a few secrets embedded into the design, as well as possible signs and symbols engraved at set points and how my Drone may be able to pick up on these at the higher levels of the building. He also knew of the tales of William Wallace's arm and the exact spot it was said to be buried. Fascinating!

The usual protocols were adhered too at this location, and I quickly gathered all the visual documentation for the files, which took a little longer here due to the vast amount of grounds to walk. The environmental data here was very much stable too; I had nothing on the equipment to suggest anything was manifesting around me while I wandered the grounds purposefully. This was likewise for both visits. The audio was, of course, more of interest even if a little quieter than other locations. The catches of note were:

"Bill Hates"
"Clear Day Destroy"
"Don't Kill Us"
"Forsaken" &
"He Knows Me."

The feeling while analysing the audio was one of a location that has seen some battle or perhaps the inhabitants had. Certainly, a look at the history would suggest this to match rather nicely to the profile. Maybe we have religious monks still wandering this location, and if so, it would not be a stretch of the imagination to think so.

You see, if we are to listen to people such as Tom Campbell about the dying process and those who are fear based when they pass, we could match perfectly why religious apparitions tend not to move far from their locals. To be conditioned through life in religion, to be told how death will play out, then discover it is not how one imagined, may cause fear and discomfort with an inability to move on from the religious location. Could this be the key to ghostly monks, nuns and such?

We shall need to keep searching to find out the answer to this and as mentioned a few times already in this book, you can follow my work freely online and perhaps even get involved and help dig that little deeper into the unknown at lovely places such as this.

Cambuskenneth Abbey
Ladysneuk Rd,
Stirling
FK9 5NG

Kirk O'Shotts

Kirk O'Shotts is located in Salsburgh, North Lanarkshire, in close proximity to the M8. Sitting in an elevated position, it is unmistakable to those travelling this area of Scotland. At night, you've most likely seen it illuminating the skyline as you make your way along one of Scotland's busiest motorways. The present church building was opened on 26th October 1821. However, we can track back previous places of worship in this area to 1450. I will hypothesise further, that most likely we would find the land has been used as a place of worship for many faiths going far back in Scotland's history.

We find such land is usually deemed as highly energetic – possibly due to ley lines – and therefore adopted as a spiritual place to say thanks and be in connection with the power source, defined by the worshipers as their creator. The Parish of Shotts has a deep covenanting history. Rev. John Livingstone, after Communion on 21st June 1630 preached a sermon in the churchyard. This spread all over Scotland and carried on for the next generation. Many of the people of the area were stout Covenanters, and some even took part in the Pentland Rising, and in the Battle of Bothwell Brig. The churchyard even boasts a historical yet tragic Martyr's Stone bearing the inscription;

"Here lies the bones of William Smith, who lived at Moremellon, who with others appeared in arms at Pentland Hills in defence of Scotland's Covenanted Word of God in opposition to popery, prelacy, and Perjury, and was murdered on his return home near this place."

Paranormal Activity.

It seems as if we have possible activity in the form of a male figure spotted on the road, where the Kirk sits. Some have speculated that this may be linked to William – the Martyr Covenanter above – as he still wanders the area. The stories currently floating around – pardon the pun - are that of a female driver who's said to have hit the Kirk O Shotts ghost. She was mortified when she got out to check and found absolutely nothing there.It was evident that the figure had mysteriously vanished into thin air.

In addition to these above stories, I regularly get communication from members of my Facebook page when I share material. This location has peaked the interest of many people who all seem to tell the same stories about the road figure.Many have heard noises in the graveyard, and the area is no secret to locals who know the gravity of the haunting all too well.

Gillian Mcneice said, "This place is freaky and I hated driving the road home past it. I'm sure I seen a ghost in the middle of the road just walk through a car."

Lorna Mcfarlane said ,"I have a very PERSONAL experience here. My brother is buried here and have had stuff done that has not an explanation. With witnesses present at the time .. xx."

My Visits

In 2006, the Scottish Paranormal team – which I founded & coordinated – captured an extraordinary piece of audio, which has never been explained satisfactorily. The audio device had been placed inside the vacant Kirk with only the Reverend sitting in a small office near the exit. The device managed to not only capture the strange sound, but it actually proceeded to turn itself off with batteries perfectly fine and tape nowhere near the end. Since then I've returned a handful of times to gather more data from the surrounding areas of the Kirk.

Although nothing physical has happened to me - well apart from a bat that flew into my head from an outbuilding, much to the hilarity of my colleagues - on a paranormal front it's relatively been quiet so far. Well, I say quiet, but this does not extend to the audio of course. We already know of the capture from within the Kirk in 2006, which sadly was lost when we closed down the old Youtube channel, but we do have updated catches. Some of the catches that stand out from here are:

"Sir Hugh"
"You Help Us"
"We Had It"
"Build Earth With Us"
"Call Out To Them All."
We also had the audio spit out, "Workmen" & "Two."

On that day two workmen were on the grounds working away. You can actually see them in my footage with the drone. This shows excellent intelligence and thus an interactive sentient spirit in the area. It's little verifications such as this that strengthens the evidence, the witnesses testimonies and shows us we are on the correct path to discovering the afterlife, and its energetic reaches into our domain.

This location can be visited freely, please just keep the neighbours in mind and leave a nice respectable reputation for us all who will no doubt return here for further discoveries.

Kirk O'Shotts (Shottskirk)
Shotts
ML7 4NT

Greyfriars Kirkyard

Greyfriars Kirkyard is the graveyard located in the heart of Edinburgh. It surrounds Greyfriars Kirk, one of the oldest surviving buildings built outside the Old Town of Edinburgh, having been begun in 1602 and completed circa 1620. The name Greyfriars comes from the Franciscan order, the "Grey Friars" who wore grey robes. Burials have been taking place here since around the late 16th century; notable Edinburgh residents are buried here at Greyfriars.

The Kirkyard is steeped in history of the Covenanters. The Covenanting movement began with the signing of the National Covenant in Greyfriars Kirk on 28 February 1638. The defeat of the militant Covenanters at Bothwell Brig around 1679, resulted in some 1200 Covenanters being imprisoned in a field to the south of the churchyard. This area is now called the Covenanters Prison, a notorious hotspot for paranormal activity.

Paranormal Activity

There is the distinctive dome shaped tomb of Sir George MacKenzie, a Scottish lawyer, Lord Advocate, essayist and legal writer, and this is a focal point for paranormal activity. In 2004 a pair of teenagers allegedly entered the tomb via a rear ventilation slot. They are said to have reached the lower vault which contained the coffins, smashed the coffins open and took a skull. Police arrived as they were allegedly playing football with the skull. The pair narrowly escaped imprisonment on the little-used but still extant charge of violation of the dead.

Covenanter's Prison has a worldwide reputation for being haunted. The malevolent spirit said to be that of the notorious 'Bluidy' George Mackenzie, who was buried there in 1691, is the prime suspect with regards to some frightening occurrences. The 'Mackenzie Poltergeist', as he is affectionately known, is alleged to be the cause of such events including, but not limited to, bruising, bites and cuts on those who come into contact. Many visitors have reported feeling strange sensations, especially dread.

My Visits

I can recall the first visit I had here clearly in my mind's eye to this day, purely due to the dread our reporter guest had on entering the area. A reporter accompanied us from The Fife Free Press, who travelled with us from Fife into Edinburgh late one Saturday night. We had a key, provided by our guide from a local tourist company who do walking tours around the town. In addition, my team were all present and raring to go at this world known location.

However, it would take mere minutes for our reporter to freak out and decide this was not for her. I felt so sorry for her; we asked if she wished to wait in the car for us to finish or till she gathered her thoughts, such was the fright she was experiencing. However, she was not happy at all. You see, she had seen what she thought was a shadowy figure crouching at the bottom of the prison. As clear as day, she was adamant that the apparition was there as if ready to pounce on anyone who would go near.

We checked the area out, but by the time we got to it, nothing was visible to us. Our reporter had enough at this stage, and we safely got her out of there. We continued with our research in the area and to be completely honest, it was a rather quiet night, if not a little strange.

I would later return here to do some filming with ITV for a feature with Annabella Weir named *Tough Gig;* this was a daytime visit where we explored the area with the famous comedian, trying to find any signs of nonphysical energies. Our search would bring nothing out the ordinary but gave us further insight into the location from behind those infamous locked gates.

In the main Kirkyard, I have conducted various environmental data collecting sessions, and we perhaps have a few energy fluctuations to report. The primary paranormal experience I can report from here was the combination of Echovox capture, EVP capture and a gifted medium who picked up the same name. Yes, a mix of three different sources for one name, given to me independently from each source.

The medium was Bryan Boyle, who managed to get the name 'Edwards' in conjunction with the same name coming through in EVP format via my camcorder of all things. I was filming Bryan doing his stuff you see and was not expecting such a capture to present itself in such circumstances. When I analysed the Echovox content at the same time, I would be shocked to discover that we had 'Edwards' come through on that too. This type of evidence is crucial and gives us a solid base to work from.

I've been contacted by many people who visit this area and have experienced the spirits of the Kirkyard. Online you will find pictures of shadows, testimonies and the above mentioned 'Edwards' video. Everyone who comes to Edinburgh and asks me for recommendations, I tell them to head to this location and wander the area with an open mind and focused on possible subtle energies. They are never disappointed, and it costs nothing to do so. This truly is a paranormal hotspot, both malevolent and subtle, a real mix of energies I feel.

Greyfriars Kirkyard
1 Greyfriars,
Edinburgh
EH1 2QQ

10. Interesting Haunts

Jedburgh Castle Jail

Built as a Howard reform prison in 1823, the impressive building that is Jedburgh Castle Jail, is the only existing example of its kind in Scotland. The museum has a display of items relating to 19th-century prison life and stunning collections relating to the history of Jedburgh. Jedburgh Castle was a 12th-century earthwork motte and bailey founded by King David I. Being in the Borders, it witnessed constant fighting between the Scottish and the English and swapped hands many times.

King Alexander III was said to have married here, and his son Alexander, Prince of Scotland was born in there in January 1264. Historically, Jedburgh certain ranks up high in Scottish history. By 1335, a stone castle with a courtyard was built on the earlier fortification, comprising the main gate and a pele tower, or peel tower, flanked by great and lesser towers.

After the Battle of Neville's Cross at Durham in 1346, the Castle passed to English ownership, and this lasted until 1409, when Robert Stewart, Duke of Albany and Regent of Scotland ordered the destruction of the fortification. Scots commanded by Sir James Douglas of Balvenie conducted the demolition.

Jedburgh Castle Jail has featured on the television programme *Most Haunted,* on which I've appeared on various occasions, to show another angle to paranormal investigation, and the Jail is a popular venue for overnight organised visits as a result. The result of this is various reports of unexplained activity by a multitude of UK investigation teams and independent researchers. This adds precious data to the already impressive paranormal files that build up to a very intriguing case.

Paranormal Activity

The Jail is said to be actively haunted by a man named Edwin McArthur, a former prisoner at the prison who was executed in

1855. It is said that his apparition has been seen threatening members of the public and causing a dark atmosphere at the place. However, he is not alone for many apparitions are seen at Jedburgh Jail, an example being the reports of a ghostly piper seen standing on the battlements. Strong presences have been felt with great regularity, and on many occasions, strange lights have also been witnessed.The Jail found itself highlighted in the media in 2005 when a paranormal investigation team experienced extreme poltergeist activity.

My Visits.

My introduction to this location was breath-taking, it reminded me so much of Inveraray Jail, yet it felt much more negative in energy. Some of the prison blocks had a dark feel to them, and I knew I was in for an interesting overnight research session.I was joined by Janice Dodds, a Trance Medium. She conducted the walk around: the whole group moved from the downstairs into the museum and across a walkway into the cell block, and then to the Bridewell and finally back to base. During this, the names Douglass and Walter were obtained.

Two sessions were conducted in the Bridewell block where guests were introduced to calling out sessions and could observe K2 EMF meters and the use of Trigger Objects and were introduced to the concepts of circle work to raise spiritual energy. During the two sessions, a plethora of experiences were observed: psychic winds blowing on hands; cold spots; being touched and pulled; the feeling of having hands touched; and general sense presences around. The sounds of groans and sighs were heard audibly, and a large number of EVPs were captured and analysed later many giving reasonable responses to the questions asked aloud. There was a significant amount of EMF activity recorded

During the investigation, there was the unusual sound of a low rumbling seemingly from the outside of the building. No apparent cause for this has been identified. There were a few small EMF spikes on the K2 meter, and guests reported the sensations of being pulled or touched, together with a watchfulness and general unease. The audio has been processed, and a number of interesting responses have been picked out. The male spirits there are incredibly hostile to women, and I would strongly suggest that women do not go into the cells alone.

I would like to share the experiences of Christopher Huff, my close colleague and extremely talented author and researcher:

I was fortunate to be invited to Jedburgh by the lovely ladies of the Gateshead Paranormal Group a few years ago. They had been to the Jail on a couple of occasions and enthused about it to me.

We arrived on a night threatening rain – there's a surprise for Scotland at about 5 pm for an investigation to last until I believe 1 am the following morning.

After a quick walk around to show the place we separated into smaller four-person group, I was in the Mixed block. It was interesting, there were a number of spirits around, children running in the corridors, and yet all was kept in order by a former gaoler who smelt of stale beer. His presence could be detected doing his rounds by the reoccurring smell of this awful stale beer

Experiments with temperature probes were interesting as the temperature was going up and down – sort of, on command. I would like to try this again sometime.

There were cold spots and spirit breezes and presences that were decidedly hostile – especially to women.

Outside in the exercise yard, a set of slabs set in a circle there was the undeniable presence of spirits walking around, and around this, possibly the boredom and tedium of this in ages past has survived to the present day.

In the Governors rooms at the top of the central building, there was an interesting moment when both another woman in the party and I began picking up on a party. There was bunting in the room and at least two young females, and on a gramophone, there was a record playing - It was Glen Miller in the mood - which dated it to WW2 although why remains a mystery.

I say that we both heard this...I asked her to describe the music without me saying anything apart from I could hear music..and she hummed In the mood...this was being played again and again as though, as soon as it had ended it was put on again.

Later in the lower floor of the central building, there was the sound of a slamming door although nobody was in the area at the time. An experiment in this area conducted by the ladies [consisted] *of asking questions with a glass and some cards showed a remarkable amount of energy around and the glass trying to launch itself off the table top.*

It was a most enjoyable investigation in a very active place....and yes it was tipping it down with rain on the way home to County Durham on the Bonneville.

You can check out more of Chris's work by searching out his fantastic trilogy of books showing a lifetime of research. As for Jedburgh Jail, I think we've experienced enough and gathered the required data to list the location as active with unexplained activity and possible interactive spirits, sentient haunting.

Jedburgh Castle Jail & Museum
Castle Gate,
Jedburgh,
Scotland
TD8 6AS

Mary Kings Close

Located in the heart of Edinburgh's Old Town, with a prime position next to the historic Royal Mile,which leads up-to Edinburgh Castle, exists a unique visitor attraction which has acquired quite a reputation for its paranormal activity. Mary Kings Close – along with the neighbouring Closes – is within the main centre of the most vibrant streets, filled with traders and residents alike. It would have been home to people, businesses, storage spaces, and the central heart of busy everyday life. This unique underground location was once named King's Close, with some historical documents also listing it as Alexander King's Close, in the days before the famous and much liked local Mary King became a resident.

In Scotland, closes and wynds were most likely named after prominent members of society. Whether this is lawyers, sheriffs or historical figures, it was seen as a great privilege to have one of these named after you. Of course, this would be mostly male members of society in those early days in Scotland's history. So for Mary King, who was a prominent businesswoman in local old town society in Edinburgh, to have the close named after her shows a great respect and status. The Royal Exchange in Edinburgh was built on top of Mary Kings Close in the 18th Century, the foundations used in the building being those which we see today as we descend underground. Mysteries, myths and folklore surround this location, and it comes as no surprise that reported sightings of spirits & ghosts are prevalent, but is Mary Kings Close really haunted?

Paranormal Activity

The Real Mary King's Close is often cited as one of the most haunted locations in Scotland, if not the world. The first filed historical sighting that we find dates back to around the 1685 period and involves the Coltheart family. The family moved into Mary Kings Close after the last outbreak of the plague that ravaged the area, and it was shortly after this that Thomas Coltheart and his wife experienced 'apparitions and unknown phantom energies' in the Close.

The files of probable paranormal activity we have of Mary Kings Close also show reported incidences that are known and not so known. These include – but are not limited to – a 'worried man' who wanders the area, a woman in black often sighted and the little girl called Annie who allegedly spoke to a famous Japanese psychic. We also have reports listing the sounds of a tavern in full swing, and scratching coming from inside a chimney, where a child sweep is said to have died. Many people can place their hand inside the chimney and often report feeling their hand being tickled or an energetic presence.

Other unusual occurrences experienced by visitors and members of staff include stones being thrown by unseen forces, unexplained footsteps walking across the wooden floors and countless recordings of voices, alarms being set off, and physical activity which may include movement of physical objects.

My Visits

I've been fortunate with my research into Scotland's most active locations, having had extensive access to Mary Kings Close between 2005 & 2008, and then a few revisits up till 2015 for various events held by the attraction. To work within the environment was a perfect opportunity to test some of the claims above personally. This then allows an informed conclusion, rather than only researching the data without stepping down into the areas. After the initial three years of research, events and personal data collection, it was a joy to work hand in hand with the attraction management in Edinburgh. Put it this way, regardless of grumbles by cynics, the data cannot be easily explained, especially by those who have never been underground in this location.

I'm on record as claiming this to be the most active location I've researched, and still, I stand by that claim. This could be due to how long I studied down there, gathering an impressive amount of data, but also due to the unique events that seemed to present themselves every visit. Mr Chesney's house, which is situated at the bottom of Mary King's Close, has been the subject of some quite intense Electronic Voice Phenomena & Echovox study over the past ten years, with some rather strange results. Personally, I've witnessed beam alarms being set off by unseen forces, I've heard footsteps walk towards me over wooden floors in the lower levels – also heard by a team of 5 researchers – and a woman's voice calling out "Hello" when the location was locked down after hours.

Cold spots are a regular phenomenon, shadow figures moving around often seen by people in the warren of rooms and various bumps and knocks have also been common during the time spent underground. I've researched a plethora of locations over the last 13 plus years, but never have I witnessed so much unexplained non-physical activity that I can personally verify as fact. Not every site looked into provides such data, personal experience, or leaves such an impression on you. Is Mary Kings Close Haunted? Yes, I would be willing to put my neck on the line here and say overwhelmingly that it is, and I know as I have had direct experience in this location.

Recent Investigations

After an absence of seven years from active research down Mary Kings Close, I returned with Mark Turner to coordinate a night of paranormal exploration with members of the public in 2014. The purpose was to allow the public to fully experience any possible paranormal activity, by a whole host of ways from spiritual practices through to equipment based techniques. I always emphasise – as does Mark Turner – that we cannot make paranormal activity manifest at such nights. What I can ensure though, is that everything that does transpire on location is 100% genuine and that if I felt it was a pointless exercise, I would not give up my time to take part in such.

A lot of work, energy, and effort goes into hosting public investigations, as each tiny detail is crucial to a free-flowing night. If there was no passion for seeking and experiencing the mysterious topic of the afterlife, you could never conduct these, as the amount of work that goes in is above and beyond what anyone could imagine. What keeps me intrigued – and pushing forward with purpose on these nights at locations – is the very thought of someone from the public having a direct experience that changes their life positively and in a contemplative way. I do not need convincing of an afterlife – or hauntings for that matter – as I've had direct experiences and know it is all authentic indeed. I could hang up my EMF Meter, Thermometers and Audio Devices right now and be satisfied that I found what I needed to in this area of reality.

So a return to one of the world most significant tourist attractions – and certainly within the top five for paranormal activity – was always going to be on the cards again, I mean, where else better to take the public to touch the paranormal so intimately? There was no way I could give up the chance to use the new Echovox audio techniques down in the Close as it has never been done before, and I love breaking forward at the leading edge of such research in such locations. We adopted a fresh approach of using an external Bluetooth speaker with an excellent audio range for live listening. This would allow us to record our sessions while also attempting communication while in the specific areas of use.

Did we hear anything out of the ordinary while in the atmospheric rooms of use? Yes, with such audio captures as "Shut up" or even more strange, asking who needs help with an immediate reply of "You" we could say we were touching upon another realm, from within the Close, that could communicate via sound waves. On the periphery of our area, while attempting communication, we often heard the very subtle movements of something unseen, something gently watching as we pushed further for communication and direct experience for the public who were taking part.

I am always mindful of the public in such sessions; it really is a game of patience, full awareness, and participation without fear. It can be long and drawn out with nothing much transpiring, or it can be intense activity, it indeed is a mixed bag. During my sessions in the location, I would say we had a mix of all this, extended periods of nothing much happening, and short bursts of audio that were well and truly beyond the scope of the software sound banks. The most exciting thing from the return to Mary Kings Close was the mediumistic session in Annie's Room, where the very talented and likeable Janice Dodds took the public into the spiritual techniques of communication with spirit.

Singing "Ring a Ring O'Roses" and then gaining the resulting high levels of fluctuating Electromagnetic energies – in tandem with what Janice was picking up vibrationally – and then adding in some sound captures, we had the perfect storm of possible activity manifesting directly for all to experience. All in all, it was a fascinating return to Mary Kings Close in Edinburgh, it was a pleasure to work with such enthusiastic members of the public as we probed this location. I genuinely feel we very subtly touched upon the afterlife via unseen energies that still seem to visit or reside within the set areas of the close.

The Real Mary King's Close
2 Warriston's Cl,
High St,
Edinburgh
EH1 1PG

Mercure Perth Hotel

The Mercure Hotel is one of the most unique locations in Perth, set in a 15th-century watermill; you can still watch the water trickling through the original water wheel from the garden, reception area and lounge bar. To my paranormally active mind – and personal hypothesis – this is the first point of interest when it comes to unseen energies and possible manifestations. I have long proposed that the medium of running water and the natural powers from such, may in fact aid paranormal activity. I cannot help but wonder if this is what creates the unexplained activity at this location in the heart of Perth.

The history of the City Mills can be traced back to 10th century with the city lade, the source of the water that you can see today flowing through the hotel as mentioned above. There is substantial evidence suggesting that it pre-dates the reign of Malcolm Canmore, who famously deposed Macbeth and married Saint Margaret of Scotland. The first mill on this site appeared around the beginning of the 12th century, and allegedly gifted to the Crown in the following century - the mills would finally be granted to the people of the city by King Robert III. Throughout the centuries the Mill is said to have suffered quite a number of fires, each time the town had to rebuild them. In the 1970s the derelict building was thankfully redeveloped as a hotel, with help from the Civic Trust scheme. The award-winning conversion has retained many of the features of the old mill.

Paranormal Activity

A ghostly apparition has been seen walking down the stairs towards the reception area, the manifestation appearing so realistic, it was asked if it wanted a cup of coffee by an unsuspecting receptionist. It allegedly answered, and then faded into the ether. The upper level, which is a stunning area with original looking beams – and items of note that would look comfortable in the old 15th Century mill – is said to have an atmosphere of intrigue, and as if some unseen energy is quietly watching.

Are these spirits related to the old mill, or is the area in general susceptible to manifestation due to the aforementioned natural energy of the water? Perhaps the items on display hold energies too, something to keep in mind. The Kinnoull Suite is also the haunt of the Hotel's resident ghost, The Green Lady. Supposedly she was a miller's daughter who hung herself from the rafters for the sake of love.

My Visits

I've been to this stunning hotel a few times now, actually staying for the weekend to soak up the atmosphere. I have to say it is one of the best hotels I've used, and the breakfast was terrific. I conducted a lot of research here with Barry Fitzgerald - known for his work on *Legend Seekers* and as a star of *Ghost Hunters International* - and we have gained a lot of useful data.I've taken a few mediums in here, and they all picked up on the girl who hanged from the overhead rafter.

Whenever we ask people to go into the particular area, without telling them the story, they all seem to pick up a feeling of dread and want to remove themselves from the area. The area is no stranger to noises either. During our first look into this building in 2014 with Barry, Lynne & Gary to name but a few, we captured a very interesting EVP saying "Mustn't Tell" (You can see it on my site)

How strange is this? \mustn't tell what? Could it be related to the girl who hung herself perhaps? On top of this, I've collected a substantial amount of audio from here with the more notable ones being:

"Annie"
"Liz"
"Bless You"
"Julie"
& "Shouldn't Be Here."

We are only just getting started with this one. Actually, I would love to have some of the readers help with the collection of data from here.

So please do check out my online places for details on how you can join us here during the festivals organised by Lynne Knight. We could use your help in getting to the bottom of this unique location for sure.

Mercure Perth Hotel
W Mill St,
Perth

PH1 5QP

The Pearce Institute

The stunning building ,which sits within Govan, was commissioned by Lady Dinah Pearce in memory of her late husband Sir William Pearce MP, and owner of the Fairfield Shipyard, who died in 1888. The building was designed by Sir Robert Rowand Anderson in the style of a large 17th-century Scottish town house and constructed between 1902 and 1906. The Pearce Institute was intended as a local social centre for the surrounding community and offered 'Govanites' separate men's and women's reading rooms, clubs, a library, a gymnasium, cooking and laundry departments, and a retiring room. In addition to this, the organ, stage and gallery in the McLeod Hall made it a popular venue for dance and social gatherings alike.

On the wall at the entrance to the building is the greeting, "This is a House of Friendship. This is a House of Service. For Families, For Lonely Folk. For the People of Govan. For the Strangers of the World. Welcome."

Paranormal Activity

The apparition of a ghostly woman has been witnessed walking across the foyer. Lights have been reported form within the building, as well as a tap that switches on by itself. On investigation sessions, we have heard tapping noises from the kitchen area within the Fairfield Room, which seems to happen very much on demand at times.

The presence of a man has been reported in the main hall on a number of occasions. On one occasion the caretaker reported hearing organ music coming from the hall, but the organ is in a decommissioned state and couldn't be played, so where did this music come from and how is this possible?

My Visits

This is a newcomer to Scottish paranormal reports by members of the public using the building. It crossed my path in 2014 and to be honest with you, I did not feel it would be as active as it has been. The Pearce Institute investigation highlights include:

- Light & Mirror was producing clear signs of manipulation by an unseen force.

The electromagnetic fluctuation was rife in the test area beside the focal audio point.

Clear knocks & thuds to the rear of the room, from walls, and from areas out-with the room.

Notable cold spots in and around people, swirling at times and not consistent.

Possible clear responses via audio – will need further analysis.

Subjective feelings of unseen energies in and around people – Various.

This was one of the more active nights, with regards to unexplainable unseen manipulation of equipment, and subjective feelings reported by individuals. The light as a prime example would fluctuate on demand at set points, the batteries were changed in the last session, and although initially, it stopped, it then proceeded to go back to form on demand.

This I would suggest was clear evidence of unexplainable phenomena witnessed by up to 30 people throughout the night. As we continue to focus on The Pearce Institute, let's look at some wider possibilities for the activity in this general area of Govan. Exactly what is the cause of the perceived paranormal activity, why is the location so attractive, and could there be some environmental possibilities for such mysteries. Purely hypothetical, but certainly as valid as any suggestions on all sides of the debate. So how about we question the ground it stands on, the nearby Govan stones, and the history of this particular part of Govan **[Further NB – apparently a well was located in the street where the PI was built, the well being located during the construction of the PI]**.

Do You Know About The Govan Stones

Govan Old Church, which has been the home of many historical places of worship going back to the 6th century, is the home of the unique collection of early medieval stones carved in the 9th – 11th centuries to commemorate the power of those who ruled the Kingdom of Strathclyde. There are 31 monuments dating from this period, including stunning carved crosses and cross shafts, along with five magnificent hogback stones. There is also the Govan Sarcophagus, the only one of its kind carved from solid stone from pre-Norman, northern Britain. **[NB – the churchyard is also said to be haunted – bit vague though on that]**

We Are All Energy

At our very root to the source of our actual being, we are all made of energy. What's more, we are strongly affected by earth & universal energies, and to dive even deeper into this area we can even hypothesis that spirit – within this vibrational plane – use such to manifest and thus come into alignment with us. It's been a long-held fact that the earth produces such energies too, and certainly, we can look at where our ancient ancestors built their places of worship, burial grounds, and other points of interest to tap into these energies.

My colleague – and future project partner – Lynne Knight of History & Horror Tours in Scotland, pointed out some key facts to me with regards to the research she has already completed on the Govan area. We suggest that this was most likely a Pagan site, and thus may in fact date back further than records show. Lynne also hypothesised about the ground the Pearce Institute sits upon, and the fact we see tunnels underneath it, cutting into the very ground! **[NB The tunnels form part of the old shooting range, but are full of asbestos. They also run beneath the churchyard, within inches of the graves]**

Earth Energies Plus Govan Stones Equal?

An abundance of raw energy. Yes, the amount housed within the stones – which was most likely worshipped and used in religious and spiritual practice – will hold this. The ground will be just as alive with it too and guess what sits in the same area and within a stone's throw – The Pearce Institute.

Whether you are a believer in ley-lines or not, there is an abundance of evidence that our ancestors did, and as such, they conducted rituals, built stone circles, places of worship, and even their own stately homes, castles, and other important structures of the times.

The energy we put out through the intentions of ritual, ceremony, and overall focus does have a direct impact on the environment of the location. We can feel the 'vibes' of such areas, we say as much, as this is purely the vibrations of left over energy which will be like a beckon to a spirit, which may or may not be earthbound.

Paranormal Activity Feeding on Energy

Yes, it is entirely hypothetical and a stretch at points, but I do feel very much that our surrounding environment – and local artefacts – can play a massive part in assisting the manifestation of spiritual activity. After all, it's energy using energy to manifest in an energetic environment! Might we see such happenings at this very attractive location?

How about ritual – yes it did and does happen – conducted on the ancient grounds, and still it seemingly holding the energies of a ceremony, earth energies, and magnified by the stored Govan Stones? There is a solid possibility for this! We are starting to get a deeper insight into this area of Govan, and we can see that many factors might be at play here.

Pearce Institute
840-860 Govan Rd
Glasgow
G51 3UU

Ruthven Barracks

Due to its strategic position within the Highlands of Scotland, this area has been the home of vital structures since 1229. This location started out life as a castle owned by Alexander Stewart, Earl of Buchan, then replaced in 1459 by a second castle, before finally being built into the rather impressive and allegedly Haunted

Ruthven Barracks. The location was constructed 1719 after the 1715 Jacobite rising.

To the rear of the barracks, we have the shell of the stables. It's well within sight of the Barracks which cast an impressive shadow of strength. The stables allowed Dragoons to patrol Wade's road what is now roughly the A9. I've mistaken this area for a church in the past due to its similar design and positioning. The impressive scenery behind the location looks towards the north, from within the stables. In times gone by, many a foe would have hidden in the surrounding hills and forests waiting for the perfect time to strike.

The whole complex comprises of two large three-storey barrack blocks occupying the two sides of the main enclosure, each block has two rooms per floor, with only the lower level accessible in its current condition

Paranormal Activity

Yes, it's rather cliché, but you do feel like you are being watched while walking around the courtyard. You may get that gut feeling to turn around – as if someone is watching – or you may even get some physical activity, which is exactly what I did while here on the 27th June 2015.

As you tour a location, gathering footage, photography & audio, you seldom contemplate that you may come face to face with physical paranormal activity. I was shocked when, as I conducted an audio gathering session while in this area, a stone landed in front of me with a loud thud. Standing in the centre of the courtyard, you know for a fact that the stone could not have fallen from anywhere. No birds were flying overhead at the time, no other visitors to the location – it was very much a mystery, which occurred right before my eyes.

The castle that once stood on this site was alleged to have been haunted by its notorious lord, who was said to be trapped in some type of time-slip limbo playing cards with a dark hooded man. Do the spirits of the Jacobites wander the grounds, or how about the once stationed soldiers? Can we hear the cries of those slain within perhaps, with the constant sieges and battles of the era to blame?

My Visits

My first visit to here would have been around 2007, as we made our way up to Culloden - via Inverness campsite - as we planned a weekend of visiting paranormal locations. This location called out to us from the main road, as it sat hauntingly, and we knew we had to spend some time there, even if only to soak up its atmosphere before we journeyed onwards. Since that initial visit, I've been another three times over several years of study into the afterlife.

I already mentioned above about having a stone thrown at me by some unseen force, a rather strange moment in time for sure. Still no answer to who, what and how though. I probed the matter on audio sessions, but nothing concrete has come through thus far. On the last visit with Fife Paranormal Research Society, now renamed Scottish Paranormal of which, I am a team member, we had a rather exciting evening here. Let's just say; it was energetic!

Our EMF meters were going off the scale, so we decided to go live to Facebook and get people involved in the craziness. It was such a great moment where lots of our online followers and friends got involved. We had done our usual baseline sweeps, and nothing was recorded. No energy sources, no unusual cold spots or anything even subtle in feeling to note. Then BANG, it just all kicked off.

We were deep within an audio session, asking many questions and looking for some answers. So we were treated to some visual acknowledgement, and some catches via sound live that we heard at the time. Also in the background at set points, we could hear a strange muffled banging noise, we never got to the source of this during the visit, but it was apparently happening in no particular pattern. Could this have been the apparitions of Ruthven Barracks making themselves known to us?

We will soon find out, as we plan to return here to gather more data from the possible energies from the afterlife.

Follow that journey online!

11. Recap of Information & Additional Information

Afterword, Information & Sources.

While compiling the information inside this book, I realised that there is so much more I could say. I found myself drawn into areas I wished to inform everyone about, subjects such as consciousness, quantum physics, the law of attraction, synchronicity and even into areas of life on other planets, dimensions and such. You see, I've found that everything is beautifully linked and the greater picture of reality and the unseen world is a deep rabbit hole indeed.

Most of these areas are far beyond the scope of this book. Initially, I would much prefer to keep to the necessary information that I feel can help a few people to do their truth-seeking and question asking .On the topic of consciousness, for example, we could easily see a plethora of chapters going into this lengthy area of research and discovery.

Perhaps in the future, we could explore the deep links between what we term as paranormal activity and the marvellous fundamental power that is consciousness. We can do so much with it, yet we have barely been taught anything in society about that spark of awareness within us all. In this book, I've tried to show what we are at the very root of our being, is precisely what we search for in the case of afterlife research and discovery. We are a spark of consciousness, some call it spirit or soul, but regardless of the metaphors used we are this unique power that is the creator of matter and not the other way around.

We need to acknowledge that the energies we seek are this too, no different, just presenting themselves in a different form. Please remember this while going on your search, be kind and respectful regardless of your belief systems.

I hope I've given good enough information in the first part of the book to show you that we are all unique on this front. I hope that I've shown that the non-physical part of us is what we look for in afterlife research and investigation. I've then condensed information with regards to methodologies, equipment, analysis and post-work to show that anyone can do this. The handy A-Z of definitions should help too, keeping you up to date with the terminology used by some in this field of research.

I've shared a handful of locations with you, some of basic information and conclusions and some with enhanced information and input from friends. You can find so much more on the main website Haunted Scotland and daily on Facebook. Bringing it all together, I genuinely hope that I've managed to provide a resource that helps the general public conduct their own research and study. Highlighting how inexpensive it should be, how easy it can be to access locations without the need for significant budgets and flashy toys.

In addition to this, I would like to openly invite you all to join us on Facebook to go deeper. Please look up the page Haunted Scotland and the group Scottish Paranormal. I would love to take some of you on location with team and me at Scottish if you're interested. More so, I want to be able to speak with you all online, so we can all grow together.

Thank you for purchasing this book, for supporting the work I do and most of all In Lak'ech (I am another you) my fellow traveller.

Please Check Out:

Haunted Scotland | www.Haunted-Scotland.co.uk
Facebook Page |
https://www.facebook.com/HauntedScotlandInvestigates
Scottish Paranormal |
https://www.facebook.com/groups/ScottishParanormal/
Spooky Isles | https://www.spookyisles.com (Writer)

Resources

Haunted Scotland
www.Haunted-Scotland.co.uk

Historic Scotland
https://www.historicenvironment.scot

Wikipedia
https://en.wikipedia.org

Tom Campbell
My Big Toe Trilogy
www.my-big-toe.com

Robert Munroe
https://www.monroeinstitute.org

Pam Reynolds
https://iands.org

Ryan Cropper
www.ryancropper.com

Christopher Huff
Haunted Second World War Airfields

Sources:

Shared stories online sent in by readers and members of Facebook, Reddit and likewise. Thank you!

All locations part of private research by Ryan O'Neill via Haunted Scotland & Scottish Paranormal

About The Author

Ryan O'Neill is a paranormal investigator, researcher and explorer into the nature of reality. He has over 14 years of experience in the field of research, specifically afterlife research and hauntings, and continues to learn and grow as the data evolves. He is the owner of Haunted Scotland, and part of Scottish Paranormal.

Ryan is recognisable from appearances on TV Shows such as Most Haunted, ITV1's Tough Gig, USA Prime-Time Show Brew Dogs (With Barry Fitzgerald & Mark Turner) along with countless radio and newspaper contributions. In addition to afterlife research and chasing unexplained phenomena throughout Scotland, Ryan also studies all aspects of consciousness, including: the power of the mind; spirituality via conscious evolution and growth; exciting topics such as The Law of Attraction; and how vibrations, energies and frequencies create our paths in life. The methodologies used by Ryan – some described within this book - consist of out-of-the-box thinking and operation and do not comfortably fit into the status-quo used by the mainstream.

It is a firm held mind-set and purpose with Ryan, which looks to cast aside the usual explanations that do not hold much water and are very rigid.

"Personal experience trumps academia if the student does not take action with an open mind. Read and repeat is easy and does not foster new thought, the basis of our education establishments, but forming a firm understanding of the world around us can only be achieved by direct experiences and takes courage and strong action." Ryan O'Neill

Printed in Poland
by Amazon Fulfillment
Poland Sp. z o.o., Wrocław